O9-BTO-033

SIDNEY LANIER

By JACK DE BELLIS

Lehigh University

 205

Twayne Publishers, Inc. :: New York

For My Mother and Father

Preface

Readers looking back at Sidney Lanier's poetry through the soft-focus lens of Romanticism see an American Victorian who made unsuitable, experimental blends of Alfred Lord Tennyson, John Keats and Edgar Allan Poe. And thus Lanier is set aside as one poet incapable of following his own direction toward Symbolist poetry, probably because his society was incapable of encouraging his development or original methods. Readers peering through a New Critic's microscope find Lanier to be an uninteresting curiosity unable to free himself from the mistaken poetical theories of his time because he committed himself to didacticism on the one hand and to excessive musicality on the other; and so he could never embody his thoughts in wit, paradox, or irony. Both readers are partially right. But, had the Romantic critics examined more carefully Lanier's aims in his "Marsh" poems or explored the kinds of musicality employed in "The Symphony," they would have been satisfied with his personal contributions to modern Symbolist techniques. Had the New Critics examined Lanier's longest poems, "The Jacquerie" and "The Marshes of Glynn," or his dialect poems, they would have found a poet whose major concepts are conveyed through paradox and irony.

Yet Lanier's work tends to leave some readers unsatisfied because it contains an unusual amount of waste. Tuberculosis, contracted in a Yankee prison camp, wasted his body; and Reconstruction poverty caused him to waste his strength writing pot-boilers. Together, tuberculosis and poverty brought about his early death. By dividing his time between music and poetry all his life, he may have robbed himself of a complete dedication to poetry. By insisting upon his intuitive, often mistaken, evaluations of major thinkers like Goethe and Kant or fellow poets like Walt Whitman and Robert Browning, Lanier rejected the help that could have shortened his apprenticeship.

But, despite the wasted strength, time, and direction, Lanier produced an enduring body of work through a lifelong struggle to find his original talent. Though he never acknowledged it as such, it was really a struggle to find the proper form in which to write. He had early found his major themes in his antebellum college essays: the pre-eminence of feeling over thought and the need to educate the feelings of his age. After several false starts, he found that the best method for such education was the creation of a highly suggestive use of nature symbols and a richly musical poetry, both of which could subtly convey the essence of Transcendental experience. By finding the esthetic shape for his ideas, he made a unique contribution to American poetry.

The aim of this study is to elucidate Lanier's work by examining its esthetic and moral complexity and thus to arrive at a proper evaluation of his place in American literature. But, since this study is an introductory one, I do not intend to make extensive relation between Lanier and his fellow writers, nor do I acknowledge more than a handful of critics or discuss in detail many of their arguments. Generally, most critics have not given Lanier the specific reading he deserves but have instead treated him historically, autobiographically, or sectionally. Thus, such New Critics as Allen Tate and Robert Penn Warren have criticized Lanier's use of musical verse as only an irresponsible way of excusing obscurity and bad metaphors, but they restricted their study to minor poems not representative of the poet at his best. Academic critics have faulted him for illogical symbolism without seeing the beauty involved in the great suggestiveness of Lanier's major symbols. And they have also praised him for contriving an allegory in his only novel, but the evidence shows that Lanier did something quite different.

In handling Lanier with relative objectivity, I have tried to pay special attention to his personal development as a poet. For this reason, I have explored in the first chapter the sources of his major themes; in the second I have traced the first literary articulation of his conflicting symbols. To clarify his synthesis of theme and technique in his major poetry, I have devoted chapters to Lanier's use of chivalry and to his maturing social consciousness. The last three chapters then interpret his chief poems, noting decisive turns in his thinking.

My other objectives are threefold: to show that Lanier's position

Preface

in American letters is solid; to answer John Gould Fletcher's question, "Just how good was he at his best, and for what reasons?";[1] and to suggest that his unique talent propelled certain aspects of the Southern Renaissance and thus helped to shape a specific identity for American literature. Lanier's most hostile critic, Allen Tate, has admitted that his poetry "has never received any very precise critical evaluations."[2] I hope that this book will make such a study possible.

JACK DE BELLIS

Lehigh University

Acknowledgments

It is a pleasure to express public appreciation for the help and encouragement this study has received. Charles R. Anderson's edition of Lanier's work, with the able assistance of many associate editors, has helped me more than I can indicate. He has given American literary scholarship a model of perceptive, thorough research.

Over many years the library staff of Johns Hopkins University has supplied numerous kind services, particularly Mrs. Frieda Thies. A grant from the Research Committee of the University of California at Los Angeles enabled me to examine the Lanier Collection at Johns Hopkins. The Institute of Research of Lehigh University has lent help in having the manuscript prepared, providing me with a talented assistant, Mrs. Margaret Fistner.

It has been my luck to have the thoughtful advice and patient criticism of my good-humored colleague, Professor Addison Bross, but ultimately whatever values this book may have are directly related to my ability to follow the patient counsel of Professor Leon Howard. The faults which remain are wholly my own.

Can I thank my wife Patricia for her patient eye and ready smile? I can try.

Contents

Contents

Chronology

In compiling this chronology I am indebted to the "Chronology" preceding volumes VII–X of *The Centennial Edition of the Works of Sidney Lanier,* edited by Charles Anderson and Aubrey Starke.

1842   Sidney Clopton Lanier born February 3 in Macon, Georgia.
1857   Entered Oglethorpe College, Midway, Georgia.
1860   Graduated from Oglethorpe with highest honor; a tutor there.
1861   May 15, first prose article published. July 10, enlisted in Macon Volunteers, stationed near Norfolk, Virginia.
1862   Fought in Seven Days' Battle near Petersburg, Virginia.
1864   Captured on a blockade runner; imprisoned at Point Lookout, Maryland. (Returned to Macon, March 15, 1865.)
1867   *Tiger-Lilies,* a novel, published. Married Mary Day.
1868   First hemorrhage and recurrence of tuberculosis.
1869   Admitted to Georgia bar. Began the "Jacquerie."
1870–   Made scattered literary contacts and musical performances
1872   while he traveled for his health.
1873   Named first flutist of the Peabody Orchestra.
1875   "Corn," published in *Lippincott's,* launched his career as poet. Contacted Bayard Taylor, James Russell Lowell, and Henry Wadsworth Longfellow. "The Symphony" published.
1876   Wrote "Cantata" for Philadelphia Centennial and "Psalm of the West." *Poems* published by Lippincott's, including only poems appearing in the magazine. Nearly died that winter.
1877   Traveled for health and employment. Played with Peabody Orchestra, December–March 1878.
1878   Wrote "Marshes of Glynn" (published, December). Begins his "Shakespeare course" at Peabody Institute and pre-

liminary studies for *The Science of English Verse* (completed, July, 1879).

1879 Lectured at Johns Hopkins University on English verse.

1880 Flutist for the Peabody Orchestra; lecturer at Johns Hopkins.

1880 *The Science of English Verse* published. Quite ill. "The New South" published. Wrote "Sunrise" and "A Ballad of Trees and the Master."

1881 Lectured at Johns Hopkins on "The English Novel." At Lynn, North Carolina, he died, September 7.

Sidney Lanier

CHAPTER *1*

The Initial Step: Lanier's Early Work

FEW writers' early influences are as easily detectable as Sidney Lanier's. Few later careers are so much a product of the focusing of many rays of interest from a spectrum of absorptions. When brought into focus in his major poems—"Corn," "The Symphony," and "The Marshes of Glynn"—those rays blend together and shed a special light upon the meaning of American literature. From the first, his unique voice would speak with an extraordinarily subtle music and a highly original imagery. Together they would seek to persuade the reader to accept Lanier's conception of emotion. But even before he began writing poetry, even long before he began writing seriously, Lanier began to synthesize all of his interests. His career reveals a remarkable unity of attitude toward the pre-eminence of feeling. And his early life shows a precocious codification of his natural inclinations and his formal training.

Lanier graduated from Oglethorpe College in 1860 with highest honor; few poets have made better use of their academic training. For at Oglethorpe he first read the major ethical philosophers and shaped his reactions to them; he first examined Thomas Carlyle's essays on German writers which stimulated the writing of Lanier's only novel, *Tiger-Lilies* (1867); he studied the English poets who later inspired him; and he continued to practice and compose music, which, in great measure, helped create the musicality of his verse. Subsequently, the Civil War and Reconstruction would add social indignation to Lanier's basic beginnings, but the source of that sensitivity can also be traced to Methodist Oglethorpe, since the school, like Lanier's curriculum, was dedicated to "the heart."

I *The Education of Feelings*

The same year Lanier left Oglethorpe, he wrote to his father about the source of the trouble between North and South: "A man must always *feel* rightly . . . before he can *think* rightly . . . the *initial step of every plan* and *every action,* is *an emotion.*" [1] He then accused the North of "unharmonious education" resulting from the "uneducated emotion" of the founder of the Black Republicans. Since, Lanier argued, the primacy of feeling would be obvious even without its biblical justification or nineteenth-century metaphysics, the North had acted against reason, tradition, history, philosophy, and God's Word. This letter sounds the note of Lanier's novel *Tiger-Lilies* and his important poetry, for it links the personal failure of a single man to a sectional failure of charity, and, ultimately ties these to "the great error of the Age." Like other poets who wished to affect the conscience of their time, Lanier would vigilantly seek out other symbolic expressions in his time that verified his idea of man's moral confusion. Additionally, he would come to recognize his own potential reflection of that need for spiritual wholeness and use his own persona as the symbol of his era's search for meaning.

Lanier had told his fraternity brothers that the education of emotions was the chief business of the nation because Northern materialism had created instability. [2] In a debate he argued that man is directly responsible for his feelings since they resulted from Adam's fall. [3] These were both rather naïve notions, of course, but they were the answering resonances in a young man to a very old philosophical position he had discovered at Oglethorpe, and to which he kept a lifelong allegiance, a tradition called the moral-sentiments tradition.

That tradition is generally thought to have originated with the writing of Anthony Cooper, who, early in the eighteenth century, championed the conception of an innate moral sense in order to refute opposed philosophers, like his student John Locke, who believed that man was solely a product of his experience. A debate raged between these differing conceptions, eventually taking the shape in America of the opposition of Empiricism and Transcendentalism, reflected in the writing of every member of the "American Renaissance," from Edgar Allan Poe to Walt Whitman.

Lanier's apparent access to this tradition was through the "Ethi-

cal Philosophy" entry in the *Encyclopaedia Britannica* by Sir
James MacIntosh.[4] This philosopher proposed a theory of innate
moral feelings, and many of Lanier's Oglethorpe writings suggest
the impact of it. "Virtue—How Distinguished from Piety," for example, offers a systematic analysis of the defects of ethical philosophers from Plato to Adam Smith.[5] Although Lanier's belief in
the importance of feeling might have led him to agree with
Smith's theory that sympathy "felt or withheld" for "the agent and
the sufferer" creates virtue, Lanier was forced to dismiss it, since
he believed that "the innate and original faculty of the soul" was
the source of moral feeling.

But the essays denouncing William Paley were the most important,[6] for Paley denied all moral sense and deduced his entire
theory from the Utilitarian duties derived from revealed religion.
Lanier rejected this theory because any philosophy which called
an act virtuous because it tended toward the greatest happiness
for the greatest number failed to make the spiritual distinction
between virtue and vice, emanating from the soul's "innate and
original faculty." This innate moral sense or innate moral feeling
could alone, Lanier seemed to feel, keep man's humanistic principles from degenerating into pragmatic relativism. In another
essay Lanier labeled Paley's belief in "the greatest good" as variable, and he rejected Paley's view that God caused man's happiness, since the goodness of God admitted free choice of action.[7]
The "right" choices were, of course, determined by "right" feelings.

II "The Error of Cousin and Hamilton"

Lanier left Oglethorpe in order to confront the consequences of
the North's "uneducated emotion" on the Virginia battlefields.
After returning to Georgia in 1865, he spent two years scrupu-
lously developing a college essay on the justification of the murder
of tyrants into "The Error of Cousin and Hamilton." [8] Sir William
Hamilton received Lanier's most serious criticism.

Hamilton, like Paley, had threatened the primacy of feeling, for
he advocated innate ideas but not innate moral feelings. His *Philosophy of the Unconditioned* (1829) in effect denied God's existence, since God, being "unconditioned," could not be known by
man's "conditioned" or limited mind. Lanier rejected this theory
because human and divine love enable relations to exist between

"the Me and the physical and metaphysical Not-Me"; thus, innate moral feelings link man and God. In closing his argument Lanier suggested that Hamilton would best be ignored.[9] The "proper metaphysician" should study the energy of love and offer the social scientist his conclusions, so they might devise methods "by which the immense power should best be educated." To illustrate, Lanier offered a rhapsodic prose-poem on the power of love, designating it "the Force of Spirit . . . in the soul, in stars, and in crystals . . . arranger of colors, of tones, and of words in what we call Art . . . and which is revealed as the other name of God."

Like Thomas Carlyle, Lanier realized that the trend in philosophy from Locke to Hamilton had been toward Empiricism rather than Transcendentalism.[10] As Lanier said at the end of "The Error of Cousin and Hamilton": "Humanity asked of philosophy a life-element, which is Love," but received instead the "death-element which is cognition." Therefore, a great philosopher was needed to lead a redirection in man's thinking. Eventually, Lanier realized that the modern poet-prophet could be that philosopher, and not only reinstitute the proper place of feeling but educate the men of his time who had mistakenly ignored the profound insights of the moral sentiments philosophers. Lanier was certain these men would respond to love if only they were educated properly. His job would be difficult. But he had a long moral tradition from which to draw strength—and he would need it.

CHAPTER 2

Symbols in Opposition in *Tiger-Lilies*

TIGER-LILIES, though Lanier's only work of fiction, was important to his development, for it gave him a chance to explore his view of the morality of feeling dramatically and symbolically, and because it offered a warning to the morally lost and the morally smug. The opposition of feeling and thought, already understood in his letter of 1860 as partly an outgrowth of Northern overeducation of intellect, became in *Tiger-Lilies* a melodramatic confrontation between humanistic Rebel Philip Sterling and satanic Yankee John Cranston. Lanier expands this conflict by revealing the different artistic and philosophical attitudes the two men represent and by offering roughly parallel scenes which contrast their attitudes toward nature. If the novel is frequently discursive, it is nevertheless securely anchored to Lanier's view that even the most knightly of Southern gentlemen can never risk becoming morally self-satisfied. The novel is both Lanier's private commonplace book of morally relevant artistic and philosophical ideas and his first attempt to exhibit the possibility of moral education through feeling on a personal and national scale.

In his preface to *Tiger-Lilies*, Lanier asserts that his interest in fiction is not to mirror life but to reveal "a love, strong as it is humble, for what is beautiful in God's Nature and in Man's Art." [1] Though Lanier occasionally intrudes into his narrative to score satiric points, he never wavers from this aim. And this goal organizes his Realistic violence as well as his Romantic meditations. A plot summary may suggest how this is accomplished.

In 1860 John Cranston and Paul Rübetsahl are guests of the John Sterlings at Thalberg, a Tennessee mansion. Cranston had seduced Rübetsahl's fiancée Ottilie in Frankfurt; and, at a masked ball, Cranston tells Paul of his misconduct and incites him to a duel. Cranston loses; and, humiliated before Philip Sterling's sister Felix whom he loves, he flees Thalberg and eventually joins the

Union Army. Book I ends as Philip falls in love with Ottilie and as war rapidly approaches. In Book II, Philip and Paul join the Rebels and save a farmer from a lynching by Negro Union soldiers. A worker from Thalberg, Gorm Smallin, has turned Yankee informer, and he joins the Unionists when his family is killed in the war. When Philip is captured in a skirmish near Petersburg, he overhears Smallin gloating over his betrayal of Paul and Philip to Cranston, who employs Smallin as his guide to Thalberg. Meeting Felix and Ottilie in the mountains, Cranston prevents Ottilie's suicide and begs Felix's forgiveness for his action at the ball. But, meanwhile, Smallin has killed old John Sterling and his wife and has burned Thalberg. Felix accuses Cranston of the crimes. In Book III Rübetsahl deserts his post to protect the women who have been escorted to Petersburg by Cranston. Philip escapes from prison and claims Ottilie, and Paul courts Felix. Cranston disappears.

As the summary suggests, Lanier was not concerned with war itself, nor did he promote a Southern bias. Instead, he used the war to examine the progress of the souls of two distinctly different men, Cranston and Sterling. To chart their progress he offers (as a poet might) a rich texture of images, related to art and nature whose analysis will clarify the principal intentions of the work and provide a deeper understanding of the development of Lanier's moral and esthetic consciousness.

I   Tiger-Lilies *and Goethe*

When Lanier modeled John Cranston, a materialistic intellectual, on Carlyle's view of Goethe's Mephistopheles, he showed more than the usual young writer's anxious search for a type to imitate.[2] Through Carlyle, Lanier learned how to concretize those errors of his age he had exposed in his essays. But despite his many references to German writing in the novel, it is unlikely that he knew any more about Goethe than he found in Carlyle's essays. The same holds true of his knowledge of Novalis or Jean Paul Richter. But his interest in German thought, his reading of Carlyle, and his work on *Tiger-Lilies* coincide and therefore offer illumination about Lanier's artistic development.

Though Lanier's Oglethorpe roommate correctly noted that, "without a doubt it was Carlyle who first enkindled in Lanier a love of German literature," [3] Lanier did not mention Carlyle until

May, 1862, when he quoted one of the essays on Richter thus: "Every sentiment and every emotion is *mad*, and exacts and builds its own world." [4] Lanier's use of Richter and Novalis in fact reveals little more than an attempt to link himself to a major strain in Romanticism. Though his editors have asserted that the German Romance fiction of Richter and Novalis influenced *Tiger-Lilies,* these authors merely helped to decorate his novel.[5] But Carlyle's essays on Goethe must have intrigued and disturbed him, for they compelled revisions in his thinking.[6]

On April 23, 1863, Lanier wrote his future wife from a Rebel bivouac: "As for that *fiendish* Göthe, he is a liar, I believe, in the sight of God!" Next day he asked her not to read Goethe for the truth, since, "Goethe is a Devil, therefore, a Liar." In 1869 he explained why Goethe lied, in such a way as to recall his college essays on the supremacy of feeling. He denounced "the wretched Goethe-doctrines of self-culture," because "That which hath to do with *Self* comes of the Devil: God is *Love,* wh. is unselfish." These ideas, Lanier insisted, were in "the *poetry* in my heart . . . before I was able to reason." [7]

Lanier's erroneous linkage of Goethe to Mephistopheles lay behind his conception of John Cranston. The creation of Cranston in turn caused some revaluation of Goethe, for Lanier admitted in 1870 that the doctrine of self-reliance was "outwardly fascinating, inwardly false," capsulizing the charm of Cranston. Though he could easily dismiss Locke, Paley, and Hamilton in his college essays, *Tiger-Lilies* showed that Lanier's creative consciousness forced a more complex understanding of the relation of thought to feeling. This deeper recognition focused Lanier's divergent interests and methods, and it gave dynamic tension to his best poetry.

Lanier shows that Cranston's selfishness was the result of his dual errors of overvaluing thought and of disparaging the redemptive possibilities of feeling. And so the charming Cranston seduced another man's fiancée, profaned music, and became blind to nature's guidance. Cranston's Romantic personality accounts for his outward charm, for in Germany he was compared to Goethe, described as having "Lucifer-eyes," and he returned invitations with poems which "breathed sweetly a satanic despair." [8] Originally, Lanier had written that the poems breathed "Werther's fiery sorrows," but in revision he chose the better comparison to Mephistopheles. Though Cranston is called creative, his

destructive urge relates him again to the devil: "A brave, nervous-
souled boy, strong of limb, strong of passion, unboundedly ener-
getic, unconquerably persevering, with an acute intellect to guide
these qualities; but thoroughly selfish, and without even the consciousness that this last was his bad trait—John Cranston was capable of building up many things; but his life was nothing more
than a continuous pulling down of all things." Cranston imagines
the world as a "wild-cat bank," issuing bills in the shape of "hypocritical men," with all virtue in the vaults embezzled by its teller;[9]
and, thus, though Lanier links him to Northern materialism, he
also shows Cranston to be critical of it, therefore, of himself.

These two descriptions of Cranston by Lanier show interesting
correspondences to Carlyle's view of Mephistopheles, for this
devil had "lynx-vision" that detected the ridiculous and bad but
was blind to nobility. He believed in the indestructible baseness
and hypocrisy of men, and "it stands written on his face that he
never loved a living soul." [10] Cynical John Cranston "had no
affaires du coeur, and he had not resolved not to have any," but
his love is entirely destructive. During his seduction of Ottilie, she
swooningly calls him Satan three times and once Mephistopheles.
His "satanic fancy" on the violin "was like a rose, with the devil
lying perdu in its red heart." John Sterling begs him to quit playing during a soiree since, "The devil's in the fiddle . . . and we'll
all be dancing a diabolical saraband."

But the last impression Lanier gives of Cranston at the book's
end more closely resembles Faust as Carlyle described him: "We
do not reckon him ill-intentioned, but misguided and miserable;
he falls into crime, not by purpose, but by accident and blindness." [11] Cranston, after all, is capable of *"affaires du coeur."* Like
a MacIntoshian "Searcher of Hearts," Lanier had found that
Cranston suffered from a mistaken life-style which could be re-
educated. Cranston may also symbolize Lanier's view of Northern
materialism. Lanier could not accept the idea of innate or pure
evil in the person or in the nation.

II *Music and Nature*

To illuminate additionally the extent of Cranston's error and
that of the age he symbolizes, Lanier contrasts his attitudes toward music and nature with that of Philip Sterling to reveal how
their moral attitudes are reflected in their sacred and profane

music. Music is the artistic expression of the state of the soul. Cranston holds his violin "as if he were strangling the poor instrument around the neck." His music reminds one of a "soul that had put out its own eyes in a fury, and gone blindly dashing about the world." This "soul" wounds itself against trees and flowers, "rising and cursing and falling again." Cranston's "dark thread" assumed "fantastic and diabolical patterns"; Cranston is thus just as much a test for Lanier's convictions about the benevolence of the emotions aroused through art as he is for the Sterlings'. By relating nature imagery to madness, Lanier shows how Cranston's music reveals his soul's rejection of Transcendental guidance. Such blindness also harms the world; and the imagery supports the concrete action.

In another place Lanier elaborates on the profane sensuousness of Cranston's music. The music he played for Ottilie was, as seen above, "a rose, with the devil lying perdu in its red heart," like a "gray eye" sparkling voluptuously, and like a star beam "hot with intoxicating perfumes." If man learns from nature, man's art can shape nature to follow his soul—an idea used in all Lanier's poetry. And so the common symbols of love (rose, eye, star) conceal man's profane nature. The image of Cranston's music as reflective of his "blind soul" has been converted to images showing a willful choice between the ethereal and the sensual. Such are the hazards of artistic inventiveness.

Cranston inhibits his own response to what he knows is the sublimest power of music—its approach to pain: "I always crush it as a sentimental weakness." But Philip Sterling rapidly quotes Emerson, Carlyle, and Richter on the "painful yearning" that beauty produces in man; and John Sterling thinks music combines all pain to an "unanalyzable yearning after God." Cranston thus rejects a path to God and would surely reject Lanier's advice to his fiancée in 1866: "Feel more, and think less! yield yourself up to the blind and vague delight of your music. . . ." [12] Yet Cranston is still vulnerable to feeling; for, when Felix Sterling sings a "prayer" to "exorcise" Cranston's "devil" (as John Sterling says), he falls under her spell and becomes dissatisfied with the role of *poète maudit*. Lanier wrote of music in a draft of his essay "Retrospects and Prospects" of 1866: "Thou beautiful Fury . . . thou Tiger-Lily of matter as Love is of Spirit." [13] But certainly his attitude toward music in his novel confirms his famous final line of "The

Symphony," "Music is Love in search of a word." Felix Sterling's music is a wordless charm which frustrates, though it does not dispel, Cranston's malevolent impulses.

Like Cranston, Philip Sterling improvises, but on the flute, which Lanier called "the instrument of the future" in "Retrospects and Prospects." [14] Philip's music is like "a rivulet shooting down smooth moss, then eddying over rough pebbles," then repeating itself—exactly the motion of the river in "The Song of the Chattahoochee" (1878). Notes weave among one another, "as the sky displays itself in patches, each with a faint star in it, through the crevices of an arabesque ruin," and "a thin clear romance" comes with a "stream of tender appealings" and a long satisfied sigh. Like "The Song of the Chattahoochee," Philip's playing has a developed complexity and tension.

The images define Philip's moral superiority, for Felix sees to the core of Philip's playing: "Music means harmony, harmony means love, and love means—God!" Cranston of course cynically rejects this relation, but Lanier certainly implies that Philip found this path to God by improvising music harmonious to nature. His love for Rübetsahl, Ottilie, and music have produced what Lanier called in his novel "the three-toned harmony our world should make." Philip resembles Carlyle's hero-poet—Lanier quoted "The Hero as Poet" in *Tiger-Lilies*—for, as Carlyle wrote, "See deep enough and you see musically; the heart of Nature being everywhere music." [15] The interlocking of music, nature, poetry, and the hero-poet remained with Lanier; Philip Sterling was his earliest symbolic union of them.

III *Nature as Moral Guide*

Lanier's reliance on Carlyle has been stressed throughout this chapter; and certainly the most emphatic, if the most general, influence of Carlyle was in his idea of the poet as hero. But, for Lanier, the poet's heroism had to be earned: from *Tiger-Lilies* to "The Marshes of Glynn" Lanier would chart the spiritual progress of his heroes as they overcame personal and circumstantial obstacles.

Though Philip Sterling is naturally optimistic, experience causes him to re-examine his assumptions by continually accepting the moral guidance of nature. In the novel's first scene, leaping over obstacles, he reaches the altarlike summit of a mountain; and the morning mist hangs like a curtain. The sun pierces the curtain and discloses the "stage" of the world with "trisky harlequins" Death and Chance: the orchestra contains half-angels, half-demons, who war with euphonious and cacaphonous music. In this "Varieties" of the universe, Heaven and Hell combat. Recognizing its dual character, Philip chooses to love nature: "since it is not possible to know thee perfectly, our only refuge is to love thee earnestly . . . and serve thee with faithful heart and stainless sword." [16] Though the view of nature is found in the earliest drafts of the novel, Philip's chivalric pledge occurs only in the published final version, suggesting that Lanier came slowly to such an affirmative view. When Philip later falls "overboard into life," he will need this chivalric pledge to sustain him.

With equal compulsion, Philip accepts Rübetsahl as his kindred spirit, imagining the mountain itself takes human form, at his friend's mysterious appearance. But Ottilie comes to the same mountains seeking a "blue ocean of loneliness." Echoing Lanier, John Sterling tells her the mountains are proof of "Christ and his purifying faculty through love"; for nature is "an infinite-tongued preacher of the Son who is our Father." But Ottilie rejects this Wordsworthian view; to her, all ideas of nature are relative. But Sterling insists: "the heart will find behind Nature love as well as terror, and will spring to the most powerful of these, which is love." Sterling does not explain what propels man to accept this Emersonian view of nature: it is an innate moral feeling, presented later in "The Marshes of Glynn."

Lanier qualifies this response to nature: the one who would be helped should have a "persistent and serious eye." Yet John Cranston seems helped even against his will. When he is insulted by Smallin's reminding him of Rübetsahl's victory, Cranston's face turns "the livid hue that makes the sea-horizon seem deadly, just before a storm." As he is about to kill Smallin, "an invisible hand" strikes him on the forehead. Cranston, confused, springs to a boulder at the mountain's peak and looks into the setting sun, a "red, flaming heart," whose "Polyphemus-eye" glares into his. As the sun sets, Cranston sees "Brown Dusk" lighting a star in the east. As a "smiling nurse" it puts the valley birds to sleep, then the "exquisite presence" stands by Cranston. He then becomes disgusted by the knowledge of his impure life and of the necessary loss of Felix.[17] His innate moral feeling, which has responded instinctively, has stymied a passionate evil action while it forced self-recognition. In fact, the description of Cranston in nature images prepares for the arrival of nature's emissary; though he wounded the sun's heart with his murderous glare, nature was still benevolent. Even if man cannot respond to what is good in nature and even if man persists in viewing it as an enemy, nature nevertheless responds to man's goodness, despite his weakness. His remorse at least brings him the first stage of conversion.

Smallin's revenge on the helpless Sterlings is a symbolic warning to all men of the harm they can do without spiritual ministry. In "The Symphony" Lanier would prophesy the coming of love even to a wasteland created by man's senseless exploitation of the land and of one another. The guidance of nature thus operates between the poles of experience and prophecy. The cynicism of Ottilie and Cranston toward the benevolence of nature has been accounted for, but what would happen to innocent Philip Sterling when he came down from the mountains to experience man's inhumanity in war?

Lanier's answer is a scene in the boat that takes Philip to prison. The boat fires a cannon at a Rebel outpost, and Philip fears a friend has been killed. He wonders: "How does God have the heart to allow it?" Seeing the indifference of nature, he responds like the hero of a Naturalistic novel: "O blind, deaf, no-hearted Beauty, we cannot woo thee . . . we cannot force thee . . . we cannot compromise with thee." He is in a quandary as he had been at the opening of the novel on the mountain top. But now no Rübetsahl settles his crisis, and chivalric submission seems impossible. Yet help is near, for a prisoner has died and on his face is the "Winged victory" of his spiritual force. Philip understands and looks seaward until the boat docks, like the speaker of "The Marshes of Glynn" who stares searchingly into the enigmatic marshes.[18]

In his moment of perception Philip Sterling stands alone as all men must, and Lanier came to see that such a man can be a moral exemplar. Though it may be impossible to love without question, the man who responds with imagination to the hazards of life will profit from nature's guidance. During a struggling apprenticeship as poet, Lanier would come to see his own career as a similar model. The education of the feelings must therefore be indirect, not didactic; eventually Lanier would find even more subtle ways to affect emotions, and his exploration of the possibilities of the musicality of verse would bring a dramatic shift to his poetic development and present him suddenly with his true voice.

Despite the general belief that the war chapters of *Tiger-Lilies* are alone of value because they place Lanier among the Realists, the scenes showing his symbolic rendering of human understanding through music and nature are more crucial to our understanding of his creative imagination. The editors of *Tiger-Lilies* correctly saw that the book is not a novel, and though it is not a German romance either, it *is* a book that projects its chief meaning through imagery and symbolism.

The pattern of Philip Sterling's awareness of love may have originated in Lanier's own disillusionment and recovery of innocence. The youthful enthusiasm leading him to write, "On to the Field of Glory!" when the Macon Volunteers moved to the front in 1861, was put to the terrible test of the Six Days' Fighting in which he helped shovel six hundred dead Yankees into the Petersburg crater. Later he nearly died of camp-contracted tuberculosis; and, after crawling home shortly before Appomattox, he witnessed his mother's death in Macon. Lanier did not withdraw from life's evil, but he tried to create an esthetic order enabling him to maintain his belief in the goodness of feeling. Having been trained at Oglethorpe to dispute those who valued thought at the expense of feeling, and having used his reading of Carlyle in writing *Tiger-Lilies* to support his poetic and melodramatic depiction of the personal and universal meaning of the conflict, Lanier was energetically establishing an internal order through his art. As he turned his talent toward poetry, relying on his understanding of the moral pattern of chivalry as the South had interpreted it, he would discover another way to create personal meaning in a world that seemed to him to be rapidly, mistakenly, becoming meaningless. He might yet discover how he could turn his rage for order outward and in educating his feelings, educate the feelings of his age.

CHAPTER *3*

Southern Knight-Errant:
Chivalry in the Early Poetry

I *"Sir Walter Scottism"*

WILLIAM GILMORE SIMMS thought Southern literature "need not feel ashamed" of *Tiger-Lilies*.[1] Had he realized what significance it had to the development of the South's most important nineteenth-century poet, he might have insisted that it was a novel to be proud of—even if *Tiger-Lilies* could not rival Northerner John De Forest's *Miss Ravenel's Conversion* as a straight war novel. Lanier's narrative impulse was obviously severely strained by his many threads of Romantic interest. In fact, the novel's story may have merely offered him an occasion for the manipulation of nature images and artistic ideas. The same might apply to his long chivalric poem, "The Jacquerie" (1868–74), for the medieval peasants' revolt allowed him once more to dramatize individual examples of moral and immoral behavior and to examine at length the symbolic meaning of man's loss of feeling and thus loss of moral direction.

As Lanier sought models to follow for his philosophical ideas (McIntosh and Carlyle) and his creation of character (Carlyle's view of Mephistopheles), so he would turn to a general tradition so rife in the South on which to harness his effulgent Romantic inclinations—the chivalric tradition, or what Mark Twain called "Sir Walter Scottism." It offered the young poet ready models in diction, setting, symbolism, and, most importantly, morality. Reactionary in their literary development, nineteenth-century Southern poets readily used archaic words; a "Camelot" conception of the medieval world; antique character types; Gothic decor or atmosphere; and an obscure idealism blended to mannered piety. Here was a third vital source of Lanier's gathering power, a tradition which would blend well with the moral sentiments, philosoph-

developing the gentleman's code in a bookish way, Lanier was seeking a standard of conduct during a time of social upheaval. More importantly, he recovered a moral rectitude that enabled him to symbolize the return of Christ as a "Gentleman" to educate the feelings of an indifferent time.

III Chivalry in the Early Poems

Lanier's early uses of chivalry were, expectedly, simply decorative. The initial line of his first poem (1859) contains archaisms and chivalric diction, and in "Spring" (1860) nature plays "Sir Walter Raleigh," an odd image also used in letters of 1867. But in "Hymn" (1861) Lanier developed a pattern of conflicting images resolved by paradox and metaphor—a controlling structure which served him well in "The Symphony." As Philip Graham has noted, Lanier showed more concern for images in opposition than did Henry Timrod, William Gilmore Simms, or Paul Hayne, perhaps reflecting thereby his sensitivity to religious dualities and perhaps given impetus by the writing of Tiger-Lilies.[22] In some ways this pattern of contrasts resembles that employed by Emerson in "Brahma" and "The Sphynx." Behind all the images in opposition is the conflict of thought and feeling which most writers of the nineteenth century shared. But few poets had felt the pull of opposing forces as early as Lanier had.

The Civil War offered an obvious subject exploiting contrasts, but six months after he returned (August, 1865) Lanier wrote "The Tournament: Joust First Being the Right Pleasant Joust betwixt Heart and Brain." The poem developed a note written the month before in his ledger: "The days of chivalry are not gone, they are only spiritualized . . . the knight of the 19th century fights, not with trenchant sword, but with trenchant soul."[23] So despite the war, Lanier followed the path of his antebellum essays, resolving the heart-brain conflict in a sequel, "Joust Second Being the Rare Joust of Love and Hate."

Each stanza of the "Joust betwixt Heart and Brain" develops a concrete contrast. Heart is "a youth in crimson and gold," while "cynical-calm" Brain is "steel-armored, dark, and cold." Heart dies, saying, "My love to my beloved!"[24] Unselfish love falls before destructive selfishness—the pattern of Tiger-Lilies and "The Jacquerie." Appropriately, Lanier published the poem in the New York Round Table, a superior magazine; but the poem was so

ical tradition, and the diverse symbolic interests sketched in Tiger-Lilies.

As John Crowe Ransom has pointed out, the South rather self-consciously patterned itself after eighteenth-century England in its grave concern for kinship, manners, gentlemanly dilettantism, code of honor, and aristocratic noblesse oblige.[2] Certainly the South's stringent attempt to retain this image in the face of impending Civil War was encouraged by the "Gothic Revival" in literature which filled libraries with versions of medieval literature.

Again Oglethorpe was formative, for Lanier had read there the most popular chivalric lore, especially Scott's work.[3] Most early critics assumed that Scott formed the "temper" or "social ideal" of the South. H. J. Eckenrode speculated, "Beyond doubt Scott gave the South its social ideal, and the South of 1860 might be not inaptly nicknamed Sir Walter Scotland."[4] Mark Twain's satires on the South, especially in Huckleberry Finn, sealed its fate with the label "Sir Walter Scottism."[5] Although Lanier accepts many of the assumptions of Scott's use of chivalry, his departures are more important than his similarities. Twain insisted that Scott created caste in the South, but Lanier's chivalric poetry developed democratic ideals, as "The Jacquerie" shows.

Lanier was never a spokesman for Scott. In all his work he mentions him only five times, glancingly alludes to him thrice. A year before his death, Lanier proclaimed that Scott "purified" the air and that "no great work in the English novel appears until we reach Scott," even though Scott's "situations" do not raise "any moral question as between man and man."[6] Had he recognized Scott's compassion for people on the periphery of life, Lanier might have found a kindred spirit. Perhaps, like Carlyle, Lanier felt Scott merely capable of the opinions and emotions of "the ordinary country gentleman."

Thus, throughout his life he was attracted to the redefined medieval code of chivalry; and a simple adaptation of antique decor and color might have facilitated a stylized withdrawal from life and marked Lanier's interest in chivalry as another example of the South's cultural lag. But more was at stake. Lanier learned to use the values of chivalry to synthesize his moral attitudes during "the tragic years" and to fashion a perspective on his age that was vital to his creative development.

II *Tournaments and Lady Worship*

Lanier entered the Civil War with a chivalric gusto which must have been typical, for Bruce Catton has observed the early war years were "almost a kind of tournament." [7] Naturally, some antebellum pageant tilts assured Southern ladies of the ability of gentlemen to "bear the sword in their behalf, if such necessity should ever arise." [8] When it did and war struck, Rebels passed the time in tournaments. Clifford Lanier described a real one in 1864 which featured the "Knight of Dixie" who rode a mule like Don Quixote's Rosinante and strolled to fetch the ring from the fence rail.[9] Lanier himself delivered an address at a tournament in 1879.[10] The Southern love of pageants lay behind the interest in these mock-jousts. And since the South saw the humor in the tilts, one might wish to discount Twain's thought that Scott bore some responsibility for the war by helping to develop Southern character. As Stephen Crane showed, both Rebel and Yankee read Scott and after 1864 discarded him.

Jousts were rather comically antique, but the cult of lady worship was as close as Lanier's own tangled courtships and so could not be taken humorously. As a Southern Victorian, his elevation of women was extraordinary, but it must be viewed in terms of his concept of the values he found inherent in women's character, which he symbolized in "The Jacquerie." As for the Southern view of women, the president of William and Mary College quoted in 1849 a statement that he thought reflected the true Southern feeling: "There is perhaps no moral power the magnitude of which swells so far beyond the grasp of calculation, as the influence of the female character." It is searching, versatile, multifarious, universal; it corrects vanity and bad taste; and it brings one's "first impressions of education." [11] For Lanier, women were repositories of moral feelings. He directed his "Confederate Memorial Address" (1870) to the women who "glorified and sanctified the Southern Confederacy!" [12]—the same women that W. J. Cash thought symbolized both Athena and the Virgin to the Southern mind. For women, the Rebels fought the war. Toasted at the one-hundredth anniversary of Georgia, woman was called "The center and circumference . . . sine, tangent and secant of all our affections!" [13] It seems likely that Lanier would have agreed, though his mature impulse was more than gyneolatry.

Lanier's view of women was partly enclosed in a genera[l] that was part of the South's "higher sentimentalism." Cliffo[rd] brother, described their relationship as "A sort of chivalry [lea]dership"; [14] and Lanier's pious respect for elders is grap[hi]shown in his observation of Robert E. Lee: "I sat down [on] grass, and gazed, with such reverence as I had never gi[ven] mortal man before." [15] An eyewitness thought Lanier eye[d Lee] with "knightly reverence as Sir Guyon or Sir Gala[had] Arthur." [16] Even after combat experience Lanier could [describe himself as a knight "keeping up the Troub[adour's?] wandering about the world with a sword at my side, and [lute] (or flute) slung on my back with the ribbon of my ladye-l[ove] Obviously, artificiality and self-consciousness did not [trouble] Lanier in his chivalric love. (Nor has it troubled his criti[cs who] have frequently called him "the Sir Galahad among our A[merican] poets.") [18]

The cult of lady worship shows clearly in all Lanier's le[tters to] women. He told his sister that the "sacredest thing" in th[e world] was "the worship which a pure man renders to a woman[," espe]cially a woman like her who had the purity of "the Wing[ed one] up Yonder." [19] An early sweetheart was called by Lanier a [saint?] like Hawthorne's Hilda. But most revealing are Lanier'[s letters] during his passionately chivalric courtship to Mary Day [Lanier]. Typically he began, "O My Queen: here am I kneeling, a[dor]ing thee," and signed his letters "Sir Philip," after Sir Ph[ilip Sid]ney, his favorite knight. Elsewhere he begs Christ to she[lter her] until he can maintain her "Queenhood and utter Royalty[." This] exaltation became faintly absurd after their wedding whe[n he] felt "an infinite yearning" for his "Christ's Ambassadress, [M]istress of Heaven." [20] Lanier later used such symbolism [in his] poetry; he already had used it in *Tiger-Lilies*.

Thus, Lanier's letters show his transforming gyneola[try into a] viable, personal ideal; for the cult of lady worship forme[d his]torical embellishment to a personal search for self. La[nier un]doubtedly would have agreed with Scott that reverent [and] courtesy toward women were the rules which gave chi[valric] essence. He told Bayard Taylor that his sonnets "In [Absence]" were part of a lifelong poem to his wife, "heart's-ease for [some] of the pure worshipfulness which dwells in the Lady t[hey cele]brate." [21] But only a fraction of his poems are love poem[s].

popular it was published in an Iowa newspaper only three months later.

But "Joust the Second," which followed in a week, is twice as long, less dramatic, and more optimistic. The Love-knight appears mysteriously: "none knew/Whether he sprang from earth or heaven," and he wears an olive branch "for grace" instead of a dagger. The Hate-knight's breath "scorched souls, as a dry drought/Withers green trees and burns them bare"—the very image of the wasteland. Like Sir William Hamilton of Lanier's philosophical essay, he is a "poor, mistaken knight." Love meets him with "heaven-heat" in his eyes and a "saintly prayer"—and Hate vanishes. The Heart-knight springs to his steed, resurrected. The Love-knight then asks the knights to replace "blood-athirst Fame" with utilitarian benevolence. The opposing elements of nature then paradoxically combine: "dove-flights sanctified the plain,/And hawk and sparrow shared a nest." [25] Love's victory has converted a basically selfish system into a religious institution, and it has also reclaimed regenerative nature from the wasteland and harmonized the opposing forces of hawk and dove. Thus, Lanier found symbolic and moral meaning in a little allegory dramatizing the emergence of humanism from barbarism. Perhaps the sounds of antique words attracted him as much as the moral conflict, but he would learn in time how to exploit the musicality of language and the symbolism of chivary to reveal his unique voice.

IV   *Toward "The Jacquerie"*

Before surveying Lanier's other uses of chivalric material, it is useful to examine how he began to develop a conscious understanding of his craft by recognizing his tendency to write diffuse imagery. In December, 1863, he completed "To ———," a poem with the conventional theme of growth through love. Since the work contained an unusual amount of symbolic obscurity, he instructed a friend to "read it twice" and urged another to "study" this "half allegory." In two long letters he explained that the poem had a triple meaning because the symbols of youth (dream and mist) "change places: sometimes the mist symbols a dream, sometimes the dream symbols a mist; *all* the time, *both* symbolize something *else*." Like most young poets, Lanier was excited to find he could construct a puzzle, but his awareness of a tempta-

tion to put vague effects before rendered feelings is a rare docu-
ment of his literary self-criticism. He observes that he had frequently noticed his "tendency to the diffuse style" created by a
"multitude of words to heighten the pat-ness of the image, and so
making of it rather a *conceit* than a metaphor." But he thought he
could correct this by adopting a terse style, with only three or four
feet to a line.[26]

Lanier probably felt his poem overly reliant on stock responses
shrouded in murky images and sought a critical vocabulary by
which to make his technical problems clear to himself. But his
terms are not very helpful, because he did not write conceits,
since he used personification as a continual figure allowing loose
points of contact between his images and his ideas, as Robert
Penn Warren and Allen Tate have shown.[27] Despite his self-
awareness, Lanier never learned how to counter his tendency to
"diffuse style," but in his marsh poems (1878–81) he discovered
ways to exploit his weakness by plunging into the potential obscurity of his symbols so he could emerge with an ingenious expression of the meaning of nature through extremely subjective narra-
tors.

Lanier also tested chivalric language in essays like "Retrospects
and Prospects" in which the music lover would defend music
"with sword, lance, and battle-axe." In the same essay a more appropriate chivalric image likens etherealized poetry to a knight
covered in silk.[28] Lanier's poetic imagery was not always this ingenious. The star is used as a symbol of the distant beloved in
most of the twenty-eight poems (1865–68). A surprisingly witty
poem "Lines Tangled about the Round Table" (1866) written for
the *Round Table* is a melee of chivalry puns. And "A Birthday
Song to S. G." (1866) is a dream-allegory in medieval style.

Chivalry served to control Lanier's language and thoughts
while his social consciousness developed. He was not to forget it,
and the lexicon of archaisms in his poetry testifies to his continued
search for an antique flavor for his thoughts. Naturally one might
be led to assume he "escaped" to another world and time, but
Lanier was no Miniver Cheevy. He used chivalric material to gain
perspective on his own time and on the future of his nation, if it
was to have one. His major work shows a deepening sense of the
modern knight as an armed transcendentalist reinstituting values
embedded in the humanistic sides of chivalry—values which "The

Jacquerie" exposes as having once fallen far short of its perhaps impossible dream.

V *"The Jacquerie"*

In writing "The Jacquerie" Lanier discovered what most users of historical images soon see: that the past may be used to reveal the inadequacies of the present. Mark Twain, for example, exaggerated nineteenth-century ills by placing them in King Arthur's time. And so in 1868 Lanier told his brother that his "novel in verse" founded on the "remarkable popular insurrection" of 1359 "in the height of *Chivalry*," was a subject "so beautiful . . . I can scarcely think of aught else." [29] His reading of Froissart at first led him to side with the privileged orders against the peasants, but he felt "terribly crippled" by this biased view; and, after reading Michelet's view of the revolt as the quashing of a social reform movement, he found his real view of it. Michelet's idea allowed him to uncover the reasons for the misuses of *noblesse oblige* in order to revivify it. The "beautiful subject" had changed before his eyes to something worthy of poetic treatment, and Lanier turned away from the glamor of chivalry depicted in Tennyson to reconsider its human meaning, as Scott had. Chivalry, like the nineteenth century, contained a great error—but it was a correctable one.

Lanier came to agree with Scott that "the generosity and gallantry" of chivalry could deteriorate into "madness and absurdity," [30] even though, as Lanier read in G. P. R. James, chivalry was "the most glorious institution that man himself ever devised." [31] He shared Scott's regret that the intentions of chivary disintegrated into "bigotry, persecution, and intolerance." Unlike its modern descendant, Northern industrialism, chivalry had shown "generosity"; therefore, Lanier could not make a real analogy between Reconstruction and the conditions before the Jacquerie. External conditions thus modified his subjective recognitions, and Lanier found chivalry could be used as a symbolic device to dramatize the conflicts of feeling and thought, heart and brain, love and hate. Chivalry failed, in Lanier's view, because knights became unable to love. Yet a loving knight, arising from the peasants who were still bound directly to the land and to ancient values, could find the words to a charm that might break the spell and restore chivalry's capacity to sympathize and to give.

Though unfinished, "The Jacquerie" reveals Lanier's intentions clearly by the pattern he had developed in "The Joust betwixt Heart and Brain": a paradoxical relationship is created between opposing images which are resolved by, or culminate in, religious symbols. The narrative begins with a stark contrast muted by its fairy-tale tone: "Once on a time, a Dawn, all red and bright,/Leapt on the conquered ramparts of the Night,/And flamed, one brilliant instant, on the world." [32] This new age of re- bellion momentarily frees chivalry from its dark designs, one of which was oppression:

> Once, Famine tricked himself with ears of corn,
> And Hate strung flowers on his spikèd belt,
> And glum Revenge in silver lilies pranked him,
> And Lust put violets on his shameless front,
> And all minced forth o' the street like holiday folk
> That sally off a-field on Summer morns.

These paradoxes are followed by disturbingly Realistic images of betrayal. The mistreated hounds turn on their knights, and the falcon rebels, driving its claws into its mistress's "painted face" and "lily throat," pressing its beak into her lips, scarring her "In a most fierce and hawkish kissing." Such Naturalistic detail is not gratuitous, but is used for castigation, as in "Retrospects and Pros- pects" in which Lanier compares musical analysis to a physiolo- gist's skinning of his beloved to improve his science. In this case, the falcon is a disguise for the spiritual birds everywhere in Lanier's poetry which bring about purification sometimes against man's will. The falcon is thus a relative to the sparrow of the joust poem, the dove of "The Symphony" and to the marsh-hen of "The Marshes of Glynn." Symbolically, its function is religious, though it also functions realistically: both uses are held in suspen- sion.

Lanier then locates the cause of chivalry's decay which has forced a disruption in the natural relation of man to his hunting dog and bird. Chivalry had "flashed his sword" over the peasants at a time when "Thought was keen and hot and quick" and when "logic came not 'twixt desire and act," so that the "devil-doctrines" of selfishness, "Want-and-Take," were the only "Form of life." In those days, Trade was young and little dreamed he would "hew

down and bind old Chivalry" and turn it into "still Romance." As
a product of foolish thought, chivalry had lost its social responsibility and had been perverted to a lust for power resembling the
rampages of unbridled Reconstruction. Lanier gives ample oppor-
tunity for a reading of the poem as a conflict of North and South,
suggesting later that only the South retained a repository of love
providing a moral regeneration. Since "The Jacquerie" was written between 1868 and 1874, the poem spanned the critical time
when his social consciousness developed significantly.

The first chapter ends with an attack on the drunkenness, glut-
tony, and miserliness of Pope Innocent who staves off the revolt of
unpaid soldiers with a wassail in which his only prayer is *"Pray,
drink."* Both the military and the church, institutions of chivalric
values, are guilty of crimes against France; but the congregation
and the foot soldiers maintain traditional values. As lords oppose
one another and as the pope and the king encourage the confusion, we witness significant desertions from the "natural" places in
the "great chain of being." The similar use of oppositions in *Tiger-
Lilies* has been richly extended from the rather routine rejections
of roles by Cranston and Smallin.

Chapter 2 ushers in the spokesman against injustice, the Fran-
ciscan friar John de Rochetaillade, who is admired by Gris Grillon,
a casualty from Poitiers, because the monk "is not fat, and loves
not wine, and fasts. . . . And threats the knights and thunders at
the Pope." The friar sees Grillon as a symbol of France since he is
a quadruple amputee. In this section Lanier thus balances the
moral, realistic, and symbolic in rough blank verse of Browningesque power. It seems clear from this section that chivalric
imagery and narrative form helped to subdue his tendency toward obscure, diffuse imagery.

When the friar quotes the "second seal" passage of Revelations
as the text for his sermon on the French martyrs, his sermon becomes a thundering arraignment of war, and he prophesies horrors for the "cold chambers of the future"; like Savonarola, he calls
for a "vast undoing of things." The friar is the first of Lanier's
"Great" men (as he called them in 1874) who challenge a corrupt
world. Eventually Lanier came to regard himself as the "Great
man" and even to identify with Christ. However, an autobiographical reading of "The Jacquerie" should not supplant esthetic
understandings of Lanier's use of imagery and paradox, although

it should suggest how personally he felt the tension which produced the poem.

In the first of two prophecies, the friar graphically depicts the fall of kings, with "ragged peoples" lapping their blood. Then idealized democracy comes to rule in a second vision resolving the conflict of war with a chant, as in "The Joust of Love and Hate," and as later in "The Symphony" and in "The Centennial Meditation." Again oppositional images are contrasted in the chant: "And high and low shall commune solemnly:/And stars and stone shall have free interview." A catalogue of grief follows, stringing in a series the ills of the entire society which, as in the poetry of Whitman, seems endless and encourages the reader to add to it. The pope could "lock Grief up," but he ignores the cry for help; and the friar then assaults the pope: "Thou'rt not God's Pope. Thou art the Devil's."

And now the friar adopts the dream-allegory to show how the church has forgotten time—the limitation against which man makes moral decisions, and the historical tradition which lends credence to moral authorities—and thereby ignores man's mortality. The dream is introduced by paradoxes in which "Life asleep did fancy he was Death," recalling doves of life and death as images of France in Chapter 1. When the friar ushers in "a spectre with a million heads," all of which moan *"Homeless,"* each head represents a disorder like madness or cynicism. The creature wears on its stomach a symbol of time: "a silver-gleaming thread of day/Spiral about a jet-black band of night." Lanier has created a Poe-esque image with which to condemn his own time as well as that of the friar. Recounting his meeting with the creature in his dream, the friar dreamed he called to it: *"Time hath bound/Thy body with the fibre of his hours."* The corrupt clergy thus faces doom for ignoring the risks of earthly time, and the friar explains that the heads of the beasts were sinful priests. The friar asks, if the priesthood rusts, what will the military order, which it has humanized, do? The time has come for action.

Though the friar has condemned false chivalry but not ideal chivalry, the peasants' experience with knighthood has ruined their desire to discriminate between the two. At the poem's end, the peasants are set straight, but their rejection of knighthood is made sympathetic by the entrance, in Chapter 3, of arrogant Lord Raoul: "At left hand rode his lady and at right/His fool whom he

loved better; and his bird,/His fine ger-falcon best beloved of all."
Raoul, who is a doubly mistaken man, puts sport before the fool's
cryptic entertainment, and his fool's diversions before his lady.
His knights are "loyal-stomach'd flatterers"; but, most importantly,
his fool hates him and warns him not to confront the friar since he
knows Lord Raoul will ignore his advice. The fool, Lanier's most
complex character, predicts that evil will come. This contradicts
his previous contention that fools are not prudent—but it paradoxically proves that contention, since the fool's advice is given unsel-
fishly. Evil comes, but it is, as we shall see, overcome. And so the
fool wisely prophesied the reverse of what Raoul expected. Lord
Raoul plays into his hands. Ironically, the fool admits he gave this
advice for a selfish reason: to incite Lord Raoul to a rash act. The
drama of Raoul's egoism is far more complex than Cranston's in
Tiger-Lilies, and it involves more contexts.

The fool's denunciation is our guide to meaning, for he shows
the best evaluative intellect of Lanier's medieval world: "Thou
languid, lordly, most heart-breaking Nought!/Thou bastard Zero,
that hath come to power,/Nothing's right issue falling!" Naturally,
this irony of the fool as wise man is conventional, but Lanier uses
it to confront the selfishness of perverted chivalry and also to suggest that the "bastard Zero" Robber Baron of America during the
"brown decades" is no match for a poet-prophet.

In Chapter 4, Gris Grillon, who lost his limbs defending Raoul,
accuses him of cowardice at Poitiers; the chapter is primarily a list
of Raoul's offenses. This is a structural flaw since it impedes the
action; but, as in *Tiger-Lilies*, Lanier is more interested in the
symbolic possibilities of his subject than in its revelation of character. Yet his handling of character, setting, and dialogue does
suggest he might have become a Southern Browning had he followed Browning's example. But Lanier's plans took him along a
direction entirely his own.

As in the scene in *Tiger-Lilies* in which Cranston is melodra-
matically prevented from killing Smallin, Raoul is prevented from
stabbing Gris Grillon—by Jacques Grillon, Gris's brother, who is
condemned to lose his ears since he listened to priests "That
mouth at knighthood and defile the Church." The friar had fortified his brotherly love, and now Marie saves Jacques's life in
Chapter 5. Unfortunately, Lanier's language reverts to pious plati-
tudes when she enters "still glittering with the God-shine on her!"

Raoul is stricken pale, and Gris Grillon watches her "calm smiling while he prayed/The Holy Virgin's blessing." She is the "Love-knight"; and, like that knight's victory over Hate, Marie's conquest of Lord Raoul is effortless. She resolves the opposition of selfishness and benevolence with images recalling those of Chapter 1:

> On him her eyes burned steadily
> With such gray fires of heaven-hot command
> As Dawn burns Night away with, and she held
> Her white forefinger quivering aloft
> At greatest arm's-length of her dainty arm,
> In menace sweeter than a kiss could be.

Marie, the same guide we have seen many times in Lanier's work, represents the spirit of nature, art, and morality; and, as a result of her appearance, the ear-cropper's knife fails in midslice. Her sudden appearance has hatched a spiritual rebellion rather than a bloody peasants' revolt—and Lanier has found his compromise between the opposed positions of Froissart and Michelet, for he does not side with either aristocrat or peasant. Lord Raoul gallops off "silent and most pale and strange,/Deep-wrapt in moody fits of hot and cold," for he has been shocked into spiritual recognition.

While Marie represents a reinstitution of Christian charity, Jacques Grillon is the new "great man" of knightly courage. If Marie spiritualized the revolt, the friar had allegorized the evil of the knights, which is dramatized in the near-mutilation of Jacques. Clearly, the symbolical treatment released Lanier from the evocation of the class struggle of the past for its own sake; he universalized the peasants' revolt into the timeless quest for justice and mercy. He had used the historical image as guide to meaning better than most nineteenth-century poets or novelists; and, though it encompassed points of contact to present evil, it went beyond it. A comparison with *Tiger-Lilies* may suggest that "The Jacquerie" more successfully marries Naturalism to symbolism because Lanier's growing subjectivity was characterized by unification of opposed elements.

Chivalric material had allowed Lanier to find, therefore, a special lexicon, to locate a time which offered symbols that could represent the conflict of value that underlay Reconstruction, to resist his tendency to write obscure diffuse imagery, and to begin to give point to his use of a paradox-resolution form. The poetry of 1865–68 and "The Jacquerie" did not liberate him from his didacticism or from his rhetorical embellishments which stemmed from his oratorical practices at Oglethorpe. Nor did the use of chivalry teach him to write concrete poetry, but it did provide him with correctives to many of his weaknesses and brought him closer to his impressionistic technique and to his symbolical view of nature, while it continued his interest in the etherealizing nature of exemplary persons who fight "not with trenchant sword, but with trenchant soul."

As Abel has noted, Lanier's qualified rejection of chivalry helped redirect his attitude toward it and the "Trade" that had overthrown it;[33] moreover, it also helped him clarify how such symbols could be used in "The Symphony." But "The Jacquerie" was a plateau in Lanier's development, for he never again wrote so long or so complex a poem about chivalry. Typically, he seems to have reached a conclusion and resolved to stand by it. Additionally, in his handling of iambic pentameter through several hundred lines, he had brought to a close his conventional metrics. Almost at once, after he had left "The Jacquerie" unfinished, he expanded his forms and his sense of the sounds of words in writing "Corn" and "The Symphony"; and, though each poem relies upon chivalric principles, both of these poems point the way toward the brilliant manipulations of sound and the dramatization of conflicts of soul found in the later marsh poems. Through his esthetic struggle with form and then through his resolving conflicting ideas about chivalry and the possibilities of moral behavior when revered institutions have decayed, Lanier found his true voice.

But he first had to sharpen his sense of the community in which he lived, and the social protest poems and the dialect poems of 1868–74 reveal his maturing social consciousness and his expanding concern for personal responsibility for the education of feelings.

CHAPTER 4

Poetry of Social Consciousness: 1865-1875

I *Early Essays and Etherealization*

BETWEEN 1865 and 1868 Lanier aligned himself with ethical traditions, asserted the importance of feeling over what he took to be German self-reliance, and explored the possibility of readopting the code of the knight. Since he had been concerned with the social uses of feeling from the start, his social consciousness may have in fact directed his philosophical interests. If *Tiger-Lilies* and "The Jacquerie" exemplify his social as well as esthetic sensitivity, he needed to confront more directly the obvious mistakes of Reconstruction before he could emerge as a poet capable of blending his social and artistic interests in "Corn" of 1874.

General Sherman has well described the scene to which Lanier returned after his fighting was done: "Mourning in every household, desolation written in broad characters across the whole face of their country, cities in ashes and fields laid waste." [1] No wonder Lanier lost the "stimulus" that had gotten him through the war when he returned to Macon; he was seriously ill for three months. He looked about "over the blankest world you can imagine" for a job. But he could not guess the actual state of the South in 1865—the vaporizing of property values, the loss of thousands of work animals and billions of dollars in slave labor, and the thousands starving in Atlanta. Despite a sudden prosperous boom in the autumn, probably resulting from carpetbagger exploits, the South was a morbid ruin. Indeed, it was to be 1880 before Alabama's cotton crop equalled that of 1860.

Since Lanier could not immediately grasp the plight of the South, his first work shows a comical not a critical tone. "Timeo Danaos" [2] is a short essay in Negro dialect—which Anderson calls the "pioneer, literary and linguistic," in that form. It describes an ex-slave's recognition that freedom was a false gift, for the Negroes must now support the whites, "now beggin' at our

[46]

dores." Though slight, the essay shows that Emancipation brought
problems which only people rooted in the land could assess, and it
sounds a theme of freedom that Lanier resumes in several
"Marsh" poems at the end of his life.

Early in 1866 Lanier surprisingly asserted that the war was
partly created by Southern pride "bad as blasphemy," for it had
led Southerners to imagine "in the face of all reason" that they
could each lick five Yankees. Lanier admits that Southerners had
been willing to use charity but that the nation had been governed
by selfish egotism. This essay, "Bombs from Below," [3] forms the
pattern of his protest poetry: he first criticizes Southern misjudg-
ments of feeling and then castigates Northern errors of reason.
Thus, the essay shows a direct connection to his prewar letter to
his father which symbolized North and South as intellect and feeling, respectively, and it is related to the dramatizing of this conflict in *Tiger-Lilies,* which Lanier was now preparing for publication.

Meanwhile, Lanier was becoming conscious of the South's
death-in-life status. In 1866 he described the "mortal stagnation"
of Macon as "dreamy, and drowsy. . . . The trees stand like stat-
ues . . . and the fire-flies flicker more slowly than I ever saw
them, before" [4] Lanier adds that no one dares ask about the state
of Trade; for, as we later learn in "Tyranny," Southern trade has
been killed. By 1875 in "The Symphony" Lanier would call for the
death of the intellectualized materialism of Northern trade.

In March, 1867, Lanier again pitched his voice comically as he
attacked the Sherman Bill, despite the fact that this First Reconstruction Act threatened to supersede all existing local govern-
ment with federal control. In the essay, "The Sherman Bill,"
Schmutz, the lager dealer, dies during an explosive fire as he
blames the Sherman Bill for ruining his business.[5] The essay is in
German dialect, again reminding us of Lanier's sensitivity to language. Both comedy and dialect provided some distraction from
"the infinite loneliness and desolation" that Lanier found in
Macon at the time he wrote "The Sherman Bill," but he planned a
series of such essays in which he would "enter the pathetic to
some degree." [6] Though this suggests he had some systematic protest in mind, the Sherman Bill was an insufficient literary symbol,
and the plan went unrealized. As we shall see he eventually found
a better symbol in the Senate and in trade.

But Lanier had time between March and May, 1867, to finish his most idealistic essay, "Retrospects and Prospects," which he had begun in 1865.[7] Expanding on a theory of "etherealization," discussed in *Tiger-Lilies,* which viewed all things as progressively spiritualizing, Lanier finds that, despite the war, nature is irresistibly moved toward spirituality. His illustrations are peculiar: avalanches become dews; volcanoes, petroleum wells. The Civil War had even etherealized because its temper was an "electric instinct" rather than "intellectual persuasion"—something he allegorized in the first joust poem, later included in "The Centennial Meditation" (1876), to the chagrin of other Southerners. Politics even converted "physical tenures" (chains of slaves?) to "religious tenures." To show how the Sherman Bill and its kind had become "religious tenures," Lanier asserts that these laws resulted from "total absence of philosophical insight into the age . . . wholly at variance with the genius of the time and of the people." A few evil men had led etherealization awry from ignorance rather than from deliberate selfishness. With the South confronted by Thaddeus Stevens, Lanier had John Cranston on his mind.

II *First Social Protest*

To some extent, Lanier's first trip North in 1867 (to New York to publish *Tiger-Lilies*) focused his attitude toward the North by acquainting him with its perfidy. From the Trinity Church tower he watched the throng on Broadway "writhe and contort itself . . . as in a premature grave . . . this serpent's agony of life hissed an impotent protest."[8] He had seen only one person who had a kind heart in New York, and Lanier later learned she was an actual kin. This meeting with the little girl and a trip up the Hudson River Valley momentarily removed the bad taste of New York and enabled him to write "How Like a Grand Water-Wheel His Life Revolved" (December, 1867), celebrating Niagara's beauty and proclaiming that it would not be defiled by having its power used to spin looms. And though in "Barnacles" he poignantly complained that the past encrusted the present and paralyzed future progress, he could still hope to write a more optimistic sequel in January, 1868. But he never did, for during January he produced instead a series of bitter poems: "Tyranny," "Laughter in the Senate," "Steel in Soft Hands," "Burn the Stubble," and the pessimistic revisions of "To Our Hills." These poems reflect the sole loss of hope in his entire career. The revisions of "To Our Hills," begun late in 1867 and finished early in 1868, are therefore instructive of his swift change in attitude.[9]

Lanier had made six revisions of the poem, rare for him, finally excising all hopeful statements, such as, "Like hills, Men, lift calm heads through any woe" (unchanged in four versions) which became, finally, "Friends, blood is in the milk whereby we grow." Deleted entirely was the optimistic ending, "Stand proud! The Dawn will meet us face to face." But what he included is more significant. In earlier versions the "stainers" squelched the mourning for the "hearts that paid" (the Rebels). But in two stanzas of December, 1867, Lanier addressed the stainers as acting with a "coward hand/Of the Northland," which enacted the spite of "dainty Senators that lagged the fight." Dramatically he concludes:

> O monstrous crime
> Of a sick Time:
> —Forever waging war that peace may be
> And serving God by cheating on bent knee
> And freeing slaves by chaining down the free.

This accusation came directly from "Retrospects and Prospects." Once more we recognize that the psychological effect of the war had been to deepen Lanier's longing for freedom. But he had changed since using this theme in "Timeo Danaos." And John Sterling's optimistic view in *Tiger-Lilies* of how man responds to goodness in nature had no place in 1868. Instead, "To Our Hills" ends with questions recalling the despair of Philip Sterling. A few clues from Lanier's life may help to explain how he came to use "the pathetic" in more than "a degree" in 1868.

III *Tyranny*

Lanier's career had reached its first crest in 1867. On March 3, he had finished *Tiger-Lilies;* in May, "Retrospects and Prospects"; by July, he had published six poems in *The Round Table,* had planned a series of essays, and was revising "The Error of Cousin and Hamilton." With "Retrospects" and "The Error" he enclosed "Infinite Solecisms" and sent them to Alabama University in an attempt to win the chair of metaphysics. But the poor cotton crop had ruined the university, and by August another project at Oakland College of Mississippi had also collapsed. So Lanier had to teach at Prattville Academy near Montgomery in the fall, and he married Mary Day in December. Despite such success in literature and in love, he began writing dark poems.

The fall of 1867 thus offers the key. Lanier had over-estimated, it seems, his interest in teaching, his stamina, and his ability to bear his separation from wife and home. Teaching so distressed him that, he wrote, "it requires all my patience, all my labor, all my ingenuity, all my art and culture and poetry and religion to withstand at all." [10] But self-pity was unlike Lanier, and he apologized three days later for being cravenhearted. However, social unrest increased his unsteady condition; for a riot erupted in Prattville in January. Lanier took his pistol, and sat "to await the enemy's charge." If these predicaments were seriocomic, Lanier's hemorrhages four days later and his darkening future at the Academy were unrelievedly grim. President Johnson's near impeachment almost forced Lanier to give up in despair, as the radicals virtually sealed the South's fate. Two days later Lanier wrote "Tyranny," which Clifford Lanier called "the nearest approach . . . yet to the present feeling of the general heart." [11]

Lanier picked up in "Tyranny" the theme of disfigured nature of "To Our Hills" and expanded it to a wasteland image: "Spring-germs, spring-germs,/I charge you by your life, go back to death." [12] The flowers cannot hide the "curse upon the hills" since man has separated himself from nature: the natural relation of the cotton mills to the land has been ruined, like the relation of the farmer to the larger community. And so Lanier declares flatly that "Young Trade is dead," and "Work" itself has sullenly bowed his head in depression. The personifications prepare us for the same device in "The Symphony," though his views of "Trade" as a symbol would change.

One of the most important things to be found in this period of Lanier's social protest is its effect on the structural organization of his poems. While the chivalric poems used paradox and reconciliation as the basic organization—one which ultimately proved most meaningful to Lanier's development—the protest poems generally group images in direct but not paradoxical confrontation; and, since there is no attempt to resolve them through religious symbolism, the sense of tension pervades the poems.

Tyranny rather than Trade was Lanier's first selection as a symbol of the errors of his century, though it was impossible to give it either freshness or force since the English Romantic poets had explored all the possibilities of the symbols of tyrant and king. Historically, the symbol would not have worked since President Andrew Johnson, the "tyrant" in 1868, had supported the Secessionist candidate John C. Breckenridge in 1860. A Jacksonian Democrat, Johnson's sympathy for the South (he had vetoed the Sherman Bill) nearly caused his impeachment at the instigation of Sumner and Stevens whom Lanier had vilified in a draft of *Tiger-Lilies*.

Of course the "tyranny" Lanier attacked was the tyranny of the Senate; and "Laughter in the Senate," [13] written three days after "Tyranny," assaulted the Senate's despotism, which had turned the South into a cripple in rags whose "heart is breaking." The sound of the merrymaking Senators' "dainty wit" associates cacophony with intellectuality, an automatic relation previously shown in Lord Raoul and John Cranston. But for the first time Lanier has generalized the crime to the entire United States Senate, and he has drawn himself away from psychological examination to allegorizing. The Senators "jibe at a wretched people's fall" but the South prepares somehow to retaliate: "a fast-rising frown/On the people's forehead lowers."

"Steel in Soft Hands," written two weeks later, uses more violent imagery to develop a sharp contrast into pathos, as the "Poor Bayonets seized by Tyranny" have crushed Lee but not Southern souls—or Southern loathing. The cowardly Senators themselves wield the weapons, and Lanier's disgust is trenchant as he limns the "rosy fingered" tyrants who grind their heels on the defeated.

Though "Burn the Stubble" has been called Lanier's bitterest poem, it ends on a clear note of hope. He calls for a war on stubble to make room for "the coming grain." The poem closes with a return to religious imagery: "O Heart, be calm, till God shall burn." The purifying fire can sear the wasteland and prepare for regeneration.

IV Raven Days

But Lanier was not yet out of the wasteland. In February, less than five weeks after writing "Tyranny," he composed his darkest poem, "Raven's Food," which was so pessimistic that the published "Raven Days" was only a third as long as the original.

Lanier's protest in "Raven Days" is created through macabre images:

> Our hearths are gone out, and our hearts are broken,
>   And but the ghosts of homes to us remain,
> And ghostly eyes and hollow sighs give token
>   From friend to friend of an unspoken pain.[14]

The many linkages of internal rhyme, assonance (ghost-token), and alliteration, especially in the first and third lines, like the feminine endings of those lines and the many aspirated *h*'s and fricative and explosive sounds all create a tone of breathlessness, longing, and reflective melancholy. Such careful use of tone color shows that Lanier's social consciousness had released a musical talent not so evident in his chivalric poems. He would later explore the hidden possibilities in such a technique to reveal the subjective states of feeling in the meditative "Corn."

These are the "Raven Days of sorrow," and the birds are asked to bring in their "whetted ivory beaks" "Some strip of sea-green dawn, some orange streaks." The intensity of the frontal vowels in "sea-green . . . streaks" contrasts to the gloomy back vowels of the recurrent line "O, Raven Days, dark Raven Days of sorrow." Though Lanier did not exploit the interesting ghosthouse symbol he had begun with, he did find a way to create a mood music that seemed appropriate to the description of the Southern wasteland. In the third stanza, the dreamlike ravens float in dusky files above the Southerners "in chains, too weak to be afraid." As in "To Our Hills," the poem ends with numb questions that stress the need for a light to touch the "mountains of to-morrow." Seven years later in "The Symphony," the situation would be exactly reversed; the bird flying over the wasteland would bring hope, not darkness.

But "Raven Days" had been created from the longer "Raven's Food."[15] Two things are interesting about the seven stanzas of "Raven's Food": five stanzas following what became the third stanza of "Raven Days" are in the chivalric vein; two stanzas following what was to be the fourth stanza of "Raven Days" completely reverse the tone of the poem. The chivalric verses echo "Tyranny," for "Work" dies when the "King" found that Work helped dispel grief. These lines are less effective and less bitter than the other stanzas, and Lanier was wise to delete them.

However, the lines at the end of "Raven's Food" were intended to answer the mournful questions of the final stanza of "Raven Days," for the ravens speak to the narrator, reminding him how Elijah was sustained by food brought by ravens: "Love grows strong on food by Ravens given,/And Grief's desired To-morrow is Love's Today." Lanier had hit on a fine idea, one that linked the poet to prophet and found spiritual meaning through the descent of a symbolic bird. But he probably omitted these lines from "Raven Days" because he found such hope untimely. Yet these lines intimate the mythic vision of the restoration of the wasteland, and it is unfortunate that Lanier could not have seen the implications.

Still, the gloom was not to be dispelled. His health worsened; and, before leaving Prattville that spring, Lanier gave another indication of his anxiety in "The Ship of Earth," which shows the world foundering without God at the helm. The "best sailors" lie among the dead—and so the young poet symbolized his situation. It is no wonder then that the new novel Lanier began that spring, "John Lockwood's Mill," [16] was never finished, despite the fact that Lanier's social consciousness was sufficiently formed for him to attempt to describe the miseries of Reconstruction in a way "so sternly realistic that no figure shall appear in it which can not be exhibited in the flesh." However, neither Lanier's heart nor his talent favored realism. The skimpy pages of "John Lockwood's Mill" echo the letters of 1866–68 and the poems of 1867–68, especially "Raven's Food."

Lanier's story had possibilities. John Lockwood and his daughter Meta (for "metaphor") make the customary opposition: Meta loves poetry; her father risks everything in land speculation. Melton, the Englishman who arranges the speculation, is a Cranston-like rationalist, and the hero modeled on Rübetsahl, Richard Roylston, instinctively dislikes him. Roylston's father had been ruined by Northern dealings in wartime; and, in a surprisingly Hawthornesque fashion, Lanier probes Roylston's guilt about his father's death. But he got no further with the novel.

By the fall of 1868, he had given up poetry and teaching for the law, had partially regained his health, and awaited his first child. With order once again in his personal life, he was able to endure the pain of the shattered world. The few poems he wrote during this time, like "Life and Song," showed he had regained his faith in etherealization. And, as he sought a reacceptance of this world after a dark night of the soul, an ironic and symbolic event took place. After speaking effectively before the Brunswick, Georgia, City Council, Lanier wondered if his talents as a "pow-wow-ist" might cheapen him into a politician. "God forbid it," he prayed, "but I am fearful." [17] Lanier would have ample practice as a lawyer in the immediate future to test his worry, and as a committed poet he could test his ability as an "unacknowledged legislator of the world." Perhaps the marshes of Glynn near Brunswick had begun to beckon.

V *Withdrawal and Counterattack*

Lanier's decision in 1868 to work in his father's law firm ended four years of substantial literary output. Between 1865 and 1869 he had written *Tiger-Lilies* and started another novel; had finished "The Error of Cousin and Hamilton," "Retrospects and Prospects," "Infinite Solecisms," and four other essays; and had composed nearly fifty poems (including most of "The Jacquerie") and twenty-eight outlines for poems. In contrast, between late 1868 and January, 1875, he wrote only one serious essay, "The Confederate Memorial Address," and seventeen poems. It seems the practice of law hampered Lanier's artistic development, but in fact it took a slightly different direction—away from criticism of the North to encouragement of the South and away from abusive or pathetic allegories toward narratives of humor and sympathy. Perhaps all but the humor were to be ingredients of Lanier's major poetry, but the excursion into dialect poetry and the pathetic or comic types of this genre provided an incubation period for his sense of the philosophical oppositions underlying social evils. Therefore, this seven-year period, though quantitatively sparse in literary production, is significant to Lanier's maturity as an artist.

Late in 1868 Lanier expanded the claims he had made for the etherealization of all things in the nineteenth century. In "Nature-Metaphors," he argued that the very use of such metaphors shows that "the immortality of spirit gains the form of matter" because of "modern love rather than modern thought." [18] Man at last had followed Christ's injunction to love his neighbors to its conclusion by now loving even "tree neighbors, river neighbors." Obviously Lanier was returning to the preprotest poems to recover his opti-

mistic roots. His dialect poems seem to proceed from a conception
similar to his view of the etherealizing quality of the nature metaphor. For foolish farmers who ignore their proper relation to the
soil need sympathetic correction by a spiritual neighbor capable
of deriving a metaphorical or symbolical understanding of their
situation. As the South's poet-prophet, Lanier tried to lead his
people from the wilderness which the errors of reason had
created.

Paul Hamilton Hayne, a fellow poet, encouraged Lanier to see
hmiself as a great poet; for, as Hayne wrote Lanier late in 1868,
in "this unfortunate *South*" there were so few men of his ability
and learning that "really you *must* do 'your devoirs' to the *uttermost*" and elevate his region in elevating himself.[19] Hayne struck a
ready will, for Lanier had already begun to conceive of himself as
the South's savior. Meanwhile, his father encouraged him to become the new Samuel Butler and ridicule the radical Republicans,
but Lanier's inclinations were not satiric, though his dialect poems
gave him the chance to discover that fact. But he wanted essentially new forms, not old models; and so, in 1870, he insisted that
the artist should "either *promulge his high, his pure, his true
thought in the forms which his particular age demands,* or, *let him
create* NEW *forms, and learn the age to appropriate and utilize
and enjoy them.*" [20] Certainly Lanier did not think his era to be as
conducive to his evangel of love as this letter suggests. But
"Corn," "The Symphony," and the "Marsh" poems show that he
meant to create new forms, just as *Tiger-Lilies* and "The
Jacquerie" had shown in their ways the same impulse. Lanier was
convinced that a modern hero could arise only in a new art form;
and, without realizing it, he became that hero as he discovered his
voice in his new forms.

Lanier's career shows a striking adherence to the role of spokesman for his age, but inevitably he could not sustain the enormous
faith in the future needed to bolster the South. In 1869, for example, in "The Furlow Masonic Female College Address," an
essay, and in "Nirvana," a poem, he fluctuated from fervent idealism to detachment. The essay encourages faith and purity against
"the hideous clamor of corruption." [21] Art and religion will triumph over "the devils of unrestraint which the war had engen-
dered." Certainly, at a female college he could not ignore the
importance of women in the future world of love and beauty, for

he insists that "Society" asks women for a Home which is a sanc-
tuary from *"all those serpents, physical, moral, political, social,
religious, that creep and crawl about the world."* If lady worship
ultimately lies behind Lanier's faith in the future, and if he is
convinced of the necessity of a great man's arrival to regenerate
the world, then chivalry is the basis of his optimism. Though the
chivalry of the South might have been artificial, it supplied Lanier
with symbols which could end the anxiety that his social awareness produced.

"Nirvana" withdraws from both the chivalric role and the social
consciousness, but it foreshadows the subjective approach of
"Corn." Writing to Hayne in 1869, Lanier anticipated the ideas of
the poem. Explaining that his powerful "sympathies" at times
plunged him into depths, he found that such moods went beyond
reason in their educative power, for they revealed a sense that a
man has *"two selves"* in which his soul looks at things "with a sort
of Before-World simplicity." The soul is "sedate as eternity," half-
amused at the struggles of the other self, knowing that "the *struggling* and *feverish self* will come out pure and whole and calm
and strong." [22] Such compartmentalizing of the social and psychic
selves must have looked attractive; but the pleasures of nirvana,
or even of noninvolvement, could never be his. Throughout the
poem, Lanier uses images in opposition but does so to promote
Olympian detachment rather than paradox. He climbs a mountain
and, unlike Wordsworth, "smiled no smile and frowned no
frown." Nothing disturbs his "calm sublime," not even art, crime,
or "fangs of snakes and lures of doves." Such serene certainty is
another criticism of "self-culture," but it does not promote education of feelings.

VI *Dialect Poetry*

More immediate matters than his writing concerned him. The
large cotton crop of 1869 revivified the error of thinking King Cotton could solve Southern problems. By 1871 the crop was one-fifth
again as great as 1860's, but Lanier saw that, if the price dropped
because of a surplus, the small farmers who borrowed on their
crops would be ruined; and more Northerners would control
Southern land. From his father's law office, Lanier witnessed some
pathetic cases of short-sightedness; and such a story became the
basis of "Thar's More in the Man Than Thar Is in the Land"

(1871), Lanier's first important dialect poem.[23] A prosperous farmer told Lanier's father in Sidney's presence how he had bought a worn-out farm from a neighbor who had then left for Texas. On returning a year later, the former owner found, to his anger, the farm regenerated. The dialect gives this little story a vividness which Lanier's novel and some of his essays had fore-shadowed. Lanier was to find that the theme of regeneration would become his most serious theme, but in these dialect poems it is treated sometimes comically.

In "Thar's More in the Man Than Thar Is in the Land," Lanier adds much in character and tone to the basic tale. Jones "lived pretty much by gittin' of loans," so his house fell into decay and "his hogs was flat as his corn-bread pones." Always in debt, he sells his thousand acres and moves to Texas, only to return five years later ruined. Brown, the purchaser, had meanwhile been hard at work planting corn and wheat, and Jones returns to find a flourishing farm. Brown gives him vittles; and, after Jones had "filled hisself and the floor," he comments: "whether men's land was rich or poor/Thar was more in the *man* than thar was in the *land*." Such "cracker barrel philosophy" typifies the dialect poems, but the rustic epigram shows that man superintends the enclosed garden and that the state of nature reflects man's nature. Pastoral values have been asserted for the first time in the cause of social amelioration. Perhaps Brown's inclusion of Jones at the supper table (not in the original story) shows the emergence of rituals of manner developed from proper relations between man and land. Jones's exploitation and desertion of the land is reprimanded, but it is enclosed within Brown's exemplary understanding. Though Lanier was barred as a Confederate from arguing in federal courts, he could fight the cotton tax with such poetry.

In "Them Ku Klux" (1871), rural common sense is celebrated.[24] The narrator shrewdly corrects Jeems Munro's mistaken ideas about the Klan. Jeems, a Yankee, had bought land from the narra-tor "when things was crinky-cranky," yet the narrator still finds him "a fust-rate honest neighbor." As a good neighbor, the narra-tor feels compelled to correct the Klan's bad press. Jeems admits his senses never revealed a Ku Kluxer, and he is astonished to hear that Sumner had accused Grant of leading a worse group. The narrator cannot find his glasses to read the article; they are on top of his head. And his own short-sightedness comically undercuts his self-satisfaction and relates him to Jeems and Sumner. But the implications of the relationship are overpowered by the simple amusement of the warm pantaloon. Dialect produces a "character" who impedes social criticism. Sympathizing with this old man as he had with Gorm Smallin in *Tiger-Lilies*, Lanier shows how his interesting individual qualities threatened to override his more serious interests. Eventually, he would discover how he could create a complex narrator and make him the center of his social and philosophical thoughts.

"Jones's Private Argument" (1871) and "9 from 8" (1871) are serious criticisms of the farmer's myopia. Jones argues that all farmers must plant corn *"and swear for true/To quit a raisin' cotton!"* [25] But the narrator overhears him reveal his true self: since cotton will fetch hard cash, Jones decides to plant all cotton. A contradiction in Jones's nature had brought on economic contradictions, which in turn would make the abundant soil into a wasteland.

The moral confusion that creates economic futility is examined in "9 from 8." [26] Like E. A. Robinson's isolatos, Lanier's Ellick Garry seeks an inner "gleam" but is frustrated. He squats "like a big bulltoad" figuring in the sand the balance of his year's work, but remorseless arithmetic shows that "Nine from Eight/Leaves nuthin' —and none to carry!" His finger writes in the sand a futile destiny; for, like Jones, he mistakenly gave fealty to King Cotton. The narrator has also planted cotton, but he has had the foresight not to mortgage his land as Garry did. Morally superior, he hollers down the road to Garry that his way of life will always leave him at the mercy of inflexible numbers, and he will have nothing to carry him through the winter. His callousness contrasts with the pathetic picture of Garry writing in the sand, which itself suggests the fate of the soil when the narrator and others exhaust it through one-crop farming.

The moral superiority of the narrator to Garry is thus questionable in the light of Lanier's other poems, and we begin to detect an irony in these dialect poems that enhances the pathos and comedy of the situations. Lanier knew that the simple temptation of money was too much for the defeated South to ignore, but he tried to reveal the moral losses involved in forsaking the natural relation of man and land. Like the later Fugitive-Agrarian writers of the 1930's, Lanier may have overly romanticized the possibilities of the small farm; for like these later writers, Lanier was not a farmer. But, like them, he saw the stupidity of allowing large companies to gobble crop liens "like snap-beans/In a patch full o' old fiel'-larks"; and he tried to suggest a more human and intelligent alternative which he later fully explored in "The New South" (1880).

Lanier's best dialect poem is "9 from 8," for the interaction of narrator and theme is complex and the scene is made to function from images that are tersely rendered. The tone is unified by irony, and a Realistic local color counters the sentimental treatment of the foolish sharecropper. Although Anderson has written that Lanier "merely amused himself with the composition of a group of verses in dialect," [27] they are deeply realized presentations of Georgia as well as interesting experiments with the peculiar music of dialect. Also, the poems formulated a way to solve the problem of diffuse imagery by encouraging concreteness, though Lanier wrote no more in dialect, sensing that he had, perhaps, exhausted its possibilities. But thematically he had begun to work with the idea of regeneration in these poems, as in his protest poems, though deeper understanding was needed before he could successfully tie this theme to the regeneration of feelings.

VII *Developing toward "Corn"*

Lanier's first major poem, "Corn," grew from Realistic and Romantic interests he had already shown. The Realistic strain is repeatedly echoed in his letters. In 1870, for example, he wrote Hayne about his disgust with the "Age of Trade." "The Confederate Memorial Address," an essay of the same year, echoed Wordsworth. "The world is far too full of noise," Lanier wrote—noise created by the worship of Trade, "the most boisterous god of all the false gods under Heaven"; bringing in its "hubbub" many evils: "Crudity, immaturity, unripeness, acidity, instability" in law, literature, society, and "self-development." [28]

Lanier's hatred of the spider web of materialism made him wave the bloody Rebel shirt and demand new heroes to support the ideals of those "good knights and stainless gentlemen." The major symbol was becoming more obvious: "trade" could unify his attack on the great errors of his age. The chief pattern of chivalric imagery was ready as his poem "Homestead" (1871) shows. The "great man" had been called, and the sense that the South

had become a spiritual wasteland had become a dominant
thought. Several important themes, motifs, and ideas had
emerged.

VIII *"Corn": Sources*

Lanier carried his first draft of "Corn" to New York when he
went there for a lung checkup in August, 1874. The second draft
was finished by October 25, but between them came "Civil
Rights," a poem which explains some of "Corn's" revisions. It relates the story of Old Uncle Johnny Stiles's unrelieved anxiety in
attempting peaceful coexistence with the Yankees; the poem is un-
matched for its violence in all of Lanier's work. Stiles had lost his
son in the war and his dam, mill, animals, watch, cotton, and corn
to Sherman. The Civil Rights Bill frustrated his hope of trying to
"treat 'em brotherlee," for the Yanks had thrown him "overboard
from off the Ship of/State." [29] As in "Laughter in the Senate," they
laugh to see if the blacks will drown the whites or vice versa.
Desperately indignant, Stiles declares that the North has forced
the South into the Hobbsean state of nature: "I tell you, Jeems, I
kin not help it—*maybe* it's a sin;/*By God! ef they don't fling a
rope, I'll push the nigger in!"* [30]

Lanier's anxiety had tested his piety as well as his optimism.
The temptation to read this poem as the rant of a bigoted old man
who resembles James Russell Lowell's Hosea Biglow should be resisted, for Stiles is certainly drawn to his conclusion against everything he believes in life. It is not merely that he thinks Southern
economy cannot support blacks and whites but that the North has
forced the races into hopeless mutual aggression against each
other. Stiles's sole error lies in his expecting the North to throw a
rope, and as Lanier had said in *Tiger-Lilies*, love is the only rope
tossed to those who have fallen overboard into life. Inevitably,
Lanier attended to the mistakes of Southern thinking about how
the South might be saved: he ushered in a "great man" in the
form of the "Corn King" who would throw the rope.

For three years before the writing of "Corn," tuberculosis made
Lanier a nomad given to "certain gloomy ideas" during his isola-
tion from his family and the garden of the South. The Texas prai-
ries, for example, brought an immense sense of loneliness. Perhaps
escaping from those "gloomy ideas" of which "Civil Rights" may
have been a product, Lanier became a professional flutist with the

Peabody Orchestra and resisted Hayne's encouragement about his "devoirs." His fellow poet called him one of the South's "few genuine men of letters" and thought Lanier's loss of interest in "The Jacquerie," "a rank injustice to our *literature*." Between 1871 and 1874 Lanier wrote only three poems and three essays. But Lanier's revulsion against materialism remained as strong as ever; for in 1872, he thanked Hayne for writing poems without commercial images. Echoing his "Confederate Memorial Address," he added: "Trade, Trade, Trade: pah, are we not all sick?" [31] Even the green alley of the woods was cloaked with the webs of trade which "conceals the Realities" of music, love, literature, charity, politics, and religion. His trips North, for reasons of health and his music career, must have fortified his awareness of the personal interference that Trade had made in his life as well as of the ugly effects it had produced in the South.

While rewriting "Corn" in New York, Lanier told his wife that the "great Artist" should have the "expressive genius of Schumann, the calm grandeur of Lee, and the human breadth of Shakespeare." This statement was symptomatic of the general sources of feeling at work in Lanier as the poem germinated, for, as we shall see, it is conceivable that the symbolic qualities for which these three artists stood were transformed in sections of the poem. Lanier was now convinced that he would become a poet in spite of (or because of) the resistance he had met. He told his wife, "A sacred fire burneth in every vein, wh. is hotter and steadier and stronger than ever before."

Preparing to be a great artist, he was also becoming more conscious of his role as the great man. He wrote to Logan Bleckley who almost alone encouraged revisions of "Corn":

. . . the splendid indignations which are also tender compassions, & which will in one moment be hurling the money-changers out of The Temple, & in the next be preaching Love to them from the steps of it:—where are we to find these? It is time for a man to arise, who is a man.[32]

In the years elapsing since Lanier had discovered that the nineteenth century was unable to use the Bible or its own metaphysical discoveries to fortify the intuitive truth that feeling precedes thought, he realized that only the return of Christ could convince his era. Since Trade, Lanier continued, "interprets the Bible . . .

guides our national & almost all our individual life with its max-
ims," its oppression on man's morality is "ten thousand times
more grievous than the worst tyrannies of the Feudal System." He
concludes: "*now* the *gentleman* . . . must arise and overthrow
Trade." Trade had overthrown Chivalry, and now a new Chivalry
would overthrow Trade. Here, by the way, was a new answer to
the dilemma he faced in "The Jacquerie" of choosing between
equally unsettling views of the peasants' revolt. But "Corn" revealed the necessity for the great man better than "The Jacquerie." With "Corn" Lanier crossed his poetic Rubicon.

IX *"Corn"*

W. D. Howells thought "Corn" too mystical and refused to publish it in *Atlantic*. *Scribner's* rejected it for its length. And so
Lanier sent it to Hayne and others for comment and thought of
publishing it as a book with illustrations, which he described to
his father as containing the chief symbols of the poem: a man
walking through the Georgia woods to a corn field; a big stalk of
corn; a red hill; and the same hill regenerated. Obviously, he was
convinced he had written something important.

In the first draft Lanier called the poem an "ode," probably
only because it followed the conventions of lofty diction and lyrical tone. Following Abraham Cowley, Frederick Tuckermann,
and Henry Timrod, he loosened the form of the ode. Following
his own inclinations, expressed in his description of the illustrated
book, he emphasized the theme of social protest. The result was a
questionable blending of fairly incompatible elements and tones,
and Lanier knew it. Therefore his revisions are of exceptional
interest.

The narrator of the first draft asserts a subjective mood at once:
"Today the woods are human; leaves caress/Like ladies' hands,
and brother boughs express/A subtlety of mighty tenderness." [33]
But we may compare this version to the richer evocation of experience in the revision of October:

> To-day the woods are trembling through and through
> With shimmering forms, that flash before my view,
> Then melt in green as dawn-stars melt in blue.
> The leaves that wave against my cheek caress
> Like women's hands; the embracing boughs express
> A subtlety of mighty tenderness.[34]

Lanier has given up the forceful metaphor "the woods are human," but probably because it lacked the idea of the Protean, evanescent changeability of nature which he preferred in the second version. The idea of this shifting, impressionistic view of nature seems intimately related to the creation of his narrator: in the first version, the static view of nature comes from a reflective narrator who abstracts himself from the scene; in the revision, the narrator inserts himself directly into the scene and transfers his impressions directly.

Though the metaphors of the leaves and the boughs have remained, Lanier has inserted more diffuse images which add kinetic shocks to the scene and suggest a mood of ecstasy. The addition of "through and through" gives a haunting sound to the first line and protracts the mood; and the changes to "trembling" and "embracing" enhance the sense of touch and also substitute three-syllable for two-syllable words. And so, along with "shimmering," they supply either an extra syllable or an elided syllable to three lines and help give greater variety to the musicality of the line. The narrator is now a rather turbulent, highly sensitized person capable of responding to the deepest meaning of nature. Like Whitman, Thoreau, and others, Lanier has responded to Emerson's command in "Nature" (1836) to go into the woods and let the spirit of the universal being flow through him. The narrator of "Corn," at least at this point, is on the way to becoming an Emersonian "transcendental eyeball."

Because Lanier detects the "beatings of a heart" in the woods, an "ecstasy of burgeoning" of the hickories is not intended to contain specific sensory experience or even an image; instead, it is intended to convey an aura of feeling which veils the other images. It is a catalytic phrase, a mark of Lanier's richer use of "diffuse imagery" which has a definite function when used in combination with musical effects, though it is obviously incapable of standing alone. Because tenuous spiritual associations touch each aspect of the woods, the entwining muscadine are locks of Jove, and the odor of the woods comes from heaven. So the narrator is automatically set to dreaming of gods and nuns as he wanders to the fence of the corn field. He has moved "up from the matted miracles of grass" where he had stopped to "pray with mosses, ferns and flowers shy," and his pantheistic passion has prepared him for a visionary experience. This symbolic journey through the woods to the essence of nature is repeated in "The Marshes of Glynn" with significant variations and deeper insight.

The "corn-captain" symbolizes "the poet-soul sublime" to the narrator, and in the October revision Lanier emphasized the chivalric nature of the corn-captain symbol and, more importantly, its role as teacher. His "every godlike sense" is "Transmuted from the four wild elements"; and so he stands as a contrasting symbol to the narrator; for the corn-captain has drawn from the variety in nature to unify it all within himself, while the narrator is dazzled by the welter of his impressions. Later in "The Marshes of Glynn," Lanier synthesizes these two possible responses to nature and experience. The corn-captain blends the "strength of earth with grace of heaven," but the narrator of "The Marshes of Glynn" makes a more difficult resolution.

As the poet unites matter and spirit, so the corn-poet synthesizes all oppositions in the manner of Lanier's "Love Knight" or Marie, rather than his "rapt Hindoo" of "Nirvana":

> So thou dost mutually leaven
> Strength of earth with grace of heaven;
>   So thou dost marry new and old
>   Into a one of higher mould;
>   So thou dost reconcile the hot and cold,
>   The dark and bright,
> And many a heart-perplexing opposite. . . .

Playing the "poet's part," it took from all so it might give to all. The corn-captain's universal good works and enormous compassion inevitably connect him to Christ; and, in the last two sections, the narrator adopts the two qualities that Lanier told Logan Bleckley the great man needed to redeem the nineteenth century: love and righteousness.

In the third section, Lanier assails the "money-changers" by denouncing the misuses Southerners had made of their land, and the fourth section extends charity to the plundered soil, as Christ had preached to the moneychangers from the temple steps. The third section reworks "Thar's More in the Man Than Thar Is in the Land" and "Jones's Private Argument," with a grim tone resembling "Civil Rights." The corn-captain rebukes the modern "Jason" for pursuing the golden fleece of King Cotton and thus erecting homes "on the shifting sand/Of trade." Such "restless-hearted children" have turned the Georgia hills into slaves, gambler's halls and abused senior citizens.

Jones deserted the hill "As barbarous folk expose their old to die." A locked-in ego, Jones "cursed his grain" and tried to exploit the land. The result was moral confusion which led him to be exploited by the confidence men of Trade. His neglect of the soil is like a "lash" on a slave's back; the fields become a "gambler's hell." The fact that neither the slave nor the hell images were in the first draft must testify to Lanier's increasing awareness of the injustice done the South by Southerners, perhaps because of the brutal struggle described in "Civil Rights." Lanier's relegation of Jones to "the oblivious West" is more final than his designation in the first draft, the "desperate" West.

Jones's demise may evoke pity, but the last section reminds us that Lanier is concerned mainly with the relation of man to land; therefore, the hills are the subject of the brief fourth section. While this space allows the narrator a prophetic vision, we miss the education of the foolish Jones's feelings—the resolution. Lanier's dialect poems had generally avoided the kind of resolution he had adopted in the chivalric poetry, but his "Marsh" poems restore it, much to the poet's advantage. It is surprising that Lanier missed the chance to describe a conversion of feelings; perhaps, since he might have been unsure how it could come about, he was content to let Jones, like Lord Raoul and John Cranston (more conscious malefactors), drift into the shadows. Lanier's decision to use pathos seriously weakened his poems and made him miss some rich opportunities.

Perhaps this sudden change occurred because of Bleckley's advice. In October, Lanier told him he had seen poetic possibilities in the number of deserted homesteads and gullied hills. In reply, Bleckley had expanded on the events of the poem and had told Lanier that his first two "pictures" were "Italian," with softness and delicacy the leading qualities. In the last two sections, he was "Flemish," Realistic. Lanier called these odd remarks "wonderfully minute, and penetrating"; but they probably misled him into overemphasizing the Realistic "Jason" section and led him to a too vigorous use of pathos through a bad conceit deriving from a literary allusion. The old hill is a "gashed and hairy Lear/Whom the divine Cordelia of the year,/E'en pitying Spring, will vainly strive to cheer." Fortunately, Lanier did not carry this anticlimactic eulogy more than eight lines: one wishes John Gould Fletcher had explained why he thought it "a stroke of genius."

At the very end of the poem, Lanier returns to the visionary narrator and salvages "Corn." He sees "golden treasuries of corn" waiting for "some bolder heart" who will regenerate the land by blending "antique sinew" to "modern art." The "antique sinew" is that of the heroic Jason and the indomitable Lear, and "modern art" derives from the impressionistic experience of nature which creates visionary states that are potentially Transcendental. In this poem the vision is so closely tied to the social protest, however, that Lanier insufficiently developed it and thus failed to make the most of the ingredients he had prepared.

W. D. Howells's rejection of "Corn" is instinctive.[35] He found its purpose and meaning mystifying; the relations between the narrative and the "apostrophes" obscure; but the "worst danger" was "a vein of mysticism." Yet Lanier's "mysticism" gives organization, meaning, and originality to his poem. Howells's preference for Realism undoubtedly led him to ignore the true direction of Lanier's talent. Lanier's treatment of the contemporary misery in the South was not actually Realistic but mythic and thus closely related to his "mysticism." His subject was not social amelioration but moral regeneration through the education of feelings. He therefore adopted the role of seer, not observer; of prophet, not witness. But the narrator takes these roles too easily, considering what he has seen: there is no sense of growth toward the complexity of the poet-prophet symbolized by the corn-captain.

Howells also overlooked the originality of the corn symbol. As Christ-like poet, the corn-captain focuses the narrator's desire to awaken and redeem his foolish people. And the symbol reveals Lanier's own desire to become the great man who could liberate his countrymen from materialism. But Lanier was virtually unknown in 1874 and the South was artistically moribund, so we can understand why Howells did not recognize that the corn section could stand alone.

Though unknown, ill, and penniless, Lanier determined to become an important poet as he carried "Corn" to unimpressed publishers while he also visited medical specialists. On October 23, nine days after receiving Bleckley's letter, Lanier told his wife that he would overcome his disappointments and become a great artist: "I *know*, through the fieriest tests of life, that I am, in soul, and shall be, in life and in utterance, a great poet." This poignant resoluteness shows a surprising self-confidence. Evidently the years in the law firm and in the health resorts and his reflections about the meaning of the social disasters of Reconstruction only sharpened Lanier's sense of obligation to educate the feelings of all men and correct the error of his time. He had called for a "great man" to drive the nineteenth-century moneychangers from the temple and preach to them from its steps. Created by circumstances which directed his deepest philosophical convictions, Lanier himself had come forward in the role. Could his art withstand the moral challenge?

CHAPTER *5*

Harmony of Themes in "The Symphony"

LOCATING himself in the "moral sentiments" philosophical tradition which elevated feeling because it assured moral responsiveness, assuming the role of a Christ-like knight which dramatized his armed Romanticism, and fulminating against the inhumanity of Reconstruction, Lanier was now ready to draw these sources of his light into a heated focus. The magnifying glass through which they would pass would be the musicality of verse demonstrated in "The Symphony." So dense are the musical effects of the poem that a detailed analysis of familiar and unfamiliar matters of prosody is indispensable. For those who feel that such an approach needs a rationale based on the conscious ruminations of the poet, Lanier was at this time preparing to write *The Science of English Verse*, a landmark work about the study of the relation of poetry to music. But it is not necessary to enter into a *post-hoc* fallacy by using the technical study as a key to the poem, for the poem itself richly rewards a study based on conventional methods. Naturally, this formal study of the poem is enclosed in the general exposition of Lanier's emotional and intellectual development, and the major new source of his development was his intense envelopment in music.

I   *Music and the Education of Feelings*

So powerful was Lanier's dedication to music that as late as 1873 he insisted that his ability in Art was "purely musical" and that he had cultivated music far more than poetry, verse being "a mere tangent." [1] We should remember that at this time in his life he had not yet committed himself to writing. Perhaps he meant to excuse as well the scanty output of poems between 1869 and 1875. Yet he was no doubt honest, for he was musically precocious, playing the violin and flute when a child. In 1863, he had composed his first work and arranged music by two composers and set

two songs by Tennyson to music. This early interest continued all
his life, taking him eventually to a serious professional career as a
performer and as a composer. He set his own poem "Little Ella"
to music in 1866, and he first performed his original composition
"Sacred Memories" in a Macon concert in 1868; but 1873 was the
real turning point; for in 1873 Lanier gave concerts for people in
San Antonio, Texas, who were "utterly astonished" at "an artist
such as the world hath not seen."

As in his poetry, technical virtuosity served the higher end of
emotional transcendence; for Lanier reported that he had only to
play three seconds to create a profound silence in his audience
and "an eerie and elfish and half uncanny mood" in himself, one
which developed such an "eloquent lamenting" that it nearly
brought tears.[2] He did not always need an audience to feel such
emotion, for he reported that he played his "Zauberflöte" alone
"fairly into a sacred frenzy" and achieved "one perfect Artist's-
hour!" Of course, his ecstasy reveals that music provided a near-
perfect withdrawal from the social problems described in previous chapters; for the letters bearing Lanier's deepest feelings
about music are conspicuously lacking in any views about contemporary affairs.

In San Antonio, Lanier composed his showpiece, "Field-Larks
and Black-birds," playing it and "Swamp Robin" in Baltimore and
New York with "stunning effect": they "fell like a bombshell in the
camp." The director of the Peabody Music Conservatory called
"Black-birds" the work of an artist, and *The New York Times*'s
music critic was "greatly stricken" by Lanier's playing. Leopold
Damrosch, a friend of Richard Wagner, declared his "Wind-Song"
was "done like an Artist," and he was "greatly astonished and
pleased with the poetry of the piece and the enthusiasm of its
rendering." Lanier told him, "I must be a musician." A distinguished flute-maker declared, "Lanier is remarkable, Lanier is
astonishing, Lanier will knock spots out of our great flautists."
And he did, for he soon gained a name for himself as a composer
while he played with the Peabody Orchestra, several Männerchor
orchestras, the orchestra of the Concordia theater, and in assorted
churches and homes. He wrote a *Gnat Symphony* for flute which
he later intended to orchestrate, and he tried to invent a larger
flute while dreaming he might expand the flute section of the orchestra. Another *New York Times* commentator found Lanier's

"Midge Dance" comparable to Berlioz's music in its "light and
brilliant structure.

Lanier continued to excite his audiences. Playing in Atlanta at
the Mozart Club, his pieces were "vigorously encored" and flowers
were rained upon him. At the Clarendon in Brooklyn, his playing
of Franz Schubert moved two girls to tears. His flute, he thought,
"would have melted the meanest heart in the land," showing that
Lanier perceived the restorative possibilities of music, for it
evoked strong feelings which, naturally, were superior to thoughts
for they were moral. The nonverbal "language" of music brought
the "content" through its "style"; and music thus overcame the
biggest problem Lanier faced as a poet: the creation of a powerful emotional form which would not merely decorate a social content didactically expressed and which would not dominate a social
theme diffusely shaped. His solution was to insist upon the identity of music and poetry and thus to wed inextricably form to
content.

Lanier seems to have made by this time an analogy between his
mystical compositions and his poetry. He had no idea that he was
among the avant-garde as a musician, but he did know the profound moral effects his music could have. However, events like his
playing before Sorosis convinced him he was a member of the
"new music," for its secretary told him nothing like his music ex-
isted outside of Wagner. Lanier was "the founder of American
music" and belonged to the "the Advance-Guard." Yet all was not
encouraging, since some audiences did not understand his music.
"When The New presents itself," he complained, "each one waits
for the other one to pronounce decisively." But only one "open
heart" could "push the good thing to heaven." [3] Therefore, it
seemed likely that a similar experimentalism in poetry could produce similar results.

Despite small setbacks, Lanier was convinced that his age was
an age of music with Wagner leading it; and, in his description of
Wagner's "Music of the Future," he suggested his own aims in
poetry, for the music seems to enable the "great and noble deeds
of time" to pass in review before the ears, rather than eyes, invit-
ing the soul to "create other processions like it." Lanier declared
exuberantly, "I would I might lead a so magnificent file of glories
into Heaven!" [4] Good moral feeling could actually be demonstrated through Wagner's music, though Lanier would have been

shocked had he taken a more careful look at the moral implications of the "Ring" cycle. (Oddly enough, "The Symphony" won
Lanier the commission to write "The Centennial Cantata" for
the 1876 Philadelphia festivities which were opened by an over-
ture Wagner wrote for the occasion.)

Lanier must have thought that he could emulate the genius of
Wagner, Berlioz, Beethoven, and Schumann for transporting
people's emotions. After his appointment to the Peabody Orchestra, he described his music's impact as "going straight to people's
hearts." And increasingly Lanier's interpretation of the music he
played had begun to resemble his musical—as well as poetical—
intentions. Ferdinand Hiller's "Dream of Xmas" thus implied "the
hearty chanting of peace and good will to men" and the "lofty
prophecies . . . of the coming reign of forgiveness and love." Of
Jacques Halévy's "Tempest" he wrote that "each note grew and
budded and opened: . . . *I* also lived these flower-tone lives."
Such descriptions suggest that Lanier's program notes are exer-
cises in self-induced transcendent states.

Naturally, a musician with Lanier's concept of music would reject classicists like Mozart, even though Mozart had written beautiful works for flute. Lanier's rejection is instructive; for, in his
description of Mozart's *Die Zauberflöte*, he relies on a stock mis-
understanding which sees the simplicity in Mozart but not the
complexity within it. Disturbed by "that poor bald music" with
"poor thin notes," Lanier asks, "Why do we cling so to humbugs?"
A more serious misinterpretation of Mozart occurs in Lanier's remarks about the tragic Symphony No. 40. Lanier finds the *An-
dante* to be "a record of sweetest confidences whispered between
the first flute and the first violins,—as if they were two young
girls just commencing a friendship!" Preciosity matches inaccu-
racy when he calls the *Finale* "a great outburst of joy." [5]

Lanier might have altered his opinion of Mozart had he read
Godfrey Weber's "On a Remarkable Passage in a Quartett by
Mozart" in his *Theory of Musical Composition*. It shows Mozart's
subtle originality in a few measures. Lanier could have referred to
it. The 1853 edition was in his library. But, as he neglected or
misread Kant and Goethe, so did he misjudge Mozart. And it is
clear by now that these were not only the impulses of immaturity
but the automatic rejections of whatever threatened his world
view—rejections necessary if he were to hold on to it and find his

personal voice. The simplicity of Mozart's style could hardly attract Lanier, for it suggested a correlative paucity of emotion; therefore, such an art would be deficient in moral power. Unfortunate as his misjudgment of Mozart was, it focuses for us the almost ruthless reductionism he pursued in order to find his surest way to educate the feelings of his age.

II *Music and Poetry: Some Observations*

Lanier was an untrained musician until rather late in life, and his letters reveal an attempt to educate his musical understanding. Sometimes anticlimax unintentionally appears: "We brought down the house, and responded to a thundering *encore* with Annie Laurie." But, generally, Lanier's letters show a conscientious attention to many things: the nature of programmatic music, the relation of music to poetry, the metaphysical and moral bases of music. Though Lanier never presented any congruent view on these matters, his comments are useful in sketching the background to his use of music in "The Symphony."

His descriptions of Berlioz's *Symphonie Fantastique* and Beethoven's *Pastorale Symphony* show that Lanier considered them "tone-poets" (part of the typical nineteenth-century interest in synthesizing the arts which later produced aspects of Symbolist and free-verse poetry). Lanier's strong preference for program music is naturally carried into his description of his own work, as he shows himself to be a fellow tone poet. In 1873, he said of "Field-larks and Black-birds" that they would be unable to know their voices from the flute's representation of them.[6] If poetry became more etherealized by imitating music, as his earlier essays argued, then music concretized as it imitated nature. From the first, Lanier's esthetic assumptions required a harmony of the oppositions of various arts with each other and of art with nature.

Though Lanier's only composition while at the Peabody was the *Gnat Symphony*, he has left the most extraordinary body of music created by a poet, although half of his twenty works have been lost—*Swamp-Robin, Field-larks and Black-birds*, and the "*Choral*" *Symphony* among them. He also left forty titled and twenty untitled musical notations and fragments. Lanier's earliest piece dates from October 22, 1863; and he noted in 1881 that he had composed parts of *The Symphony of the Woods, The Symphony of the Plantation, Symphony "Life"* and had converted his

"Psalm of the West" into a *"Choral"* Symphony.[7] The *Symphony "Life"* uses the four ages of man as subjects for its four movements, as Lanier's poem "The Symphony" personifies the oboe, flute, French horn, and bassoon, respectively, in man's four ages. All these titles show that Lanier intended to blend music and poetry by imitating the program music of his predecessors.

Lanier had always been interested in descriptive music; but he realized, like Felix Sterling, that such music "is all humbug unless you give us the idea!" This statement places the meaning of the work in the intention of the author (and, incidentally, partially protects him from hostile critics since his intent is inaccessible) and thus makes him its only true interpreter. Program music had been part of the "tone color" of music since Johann Sebastian Bach, but Lanier's insistence was in a sense extramusical in its reliance on the author's explication (like the personal program in works by most romantic composers). Naturally the program is in the music and succeeds as the music does, but Lanier appeared to think it could stand alone.

Philip Sterling was of the opinion that a professor of music should be considered one of the professors of metaphysics, and Felix put the etherealizing quality of music succinctly: "Music means harmony, harmony means love, and love means—God!" This assertion expresses Lanier's program in general for his music, and in particular for the end of his poem "The Symphony." As he noted in "Infinite Solecisms," of 1869, "Music is a whole great step nearer the infinite than poetry because it *is* less rigorously formulated." [8] Lanier could always explain his poetic flaws with this formula, but the fact that he did not renounce poetry for music shows that he wished to use the more finite content of poetry to define his ideas. Even descriptive music, after all, would always leave the artist's ideas vague. But the themes of regeneration and education were not abstract and had to be made personal to be effective.

By using the artistic form which Lanier conceived to be closest to God, he elevated the poetic thoughts of "The Symphony." All poetry is rhythmical, and Lanier found in this fact a cause for metaphysical speculation. Despite his daily exposure to the form of the symphony and his own experiments with it, Lanier probably never intended to use symphonic form in his poem. The interest that provoked him to read a novel based on Mendelssohn's

life, was probably the composer's "Prayer," which was also called
"O for the Wings of a Dove." On the other hand, Lanier was disgusted at the "infinitely lascivious and suggestive" songs of
Jacques Offenbach. But his refusal to admit that anything valuable could be found in Mozart's *Die Zauberflöte* can only be evidence of his narrow exclusiveness. (Lanier might have been
repelled by the opera's Freemasonry, since Mozart was a Free-
mason.)

Lanier's admiration for Wagner as an advocate of the "New
Music" is obviously not located in Wagner's moral content but in
his experimentalism. But because of Lanier's theory of etherealization, the two things were related in his mind. For him, orchestration represented the greatest forward stride in the New Music,
probably because it provided richer resources of emotional response and greater possibilities of harmonic inventiveness. His
own practice was not quite avant-garde, for, when orchestrating
the *Gnat Symphony*, he simply added a flute *obbligato* in the manner of Berlioz. Speaking "in advocacy of pure music," he told his
brother: "I'll never rest until I lead an Orchestra with twenty
flutes sitting opposite twenty violins." [9] The orchestra of the future that he envisioned was really performing a concerto, not a
symphony, with Lanier the soloist-conductor-composer. His poem
"The Symphony" more closely resembles a "Concerto for Orchestra" than a conventional symphony; for six instruments have solo
voices, each with different rhythms, tone colors, and themes.

III   *The Musicality of Verse*

From the beginning, Lanier had, like most poets, evinced a
sense for the musical qualities of language. But he was more acute
to matters of rhythm and rhyme than most other writers, as is
proudly indicated in his note to his first poem (1858): "Composite
metre!!" By 1869, he had used twenty different rhyme schemes,
revealing a natural desire to experiment. By the time he wrote
"Corn," he had learned to create rhythms which did not depend
upon conventional concepts of stress; instead, he used phrase and
line to develop a more original kind of music.

His letters to fellow poets John Bannister Tabb, Paul Hayne,
and Bayard Taylor include much criticism of their rhythm and
meter, while in Lanier's travel book *Florida* he too easily declared that Henry Timrod "never had time to learn the mere

craft of the poet—the technique of verse." [10] In 1871 he praised
Paul Hayne's musical sense of rhythm as "a flow of melody" un-
brokenly perfect. His essay on Hayne (1872–75) called his poetry
"essentially, thoroughly, and charmingly tuneful." Lanier coun-
seled Bayard Taylor to organize Taylor's hymn so that the first
stanza introduced three ideas, the next three enlarged on them
and the fifth summarized them, allowing the poem to end "on a
tonic." Taylor thought this "architectural structure" misapplied
"the laws of Music to Poetry"; but Lanier considered himself an
authority on the musicality of verse and, to his credit, ignored
Taylor.[11] Perhaps Lanier's arbitrary comments about the musicality of his friends' poetry (or the lack of it) compensated for his
lack of success and reaffirmed his sense of the almost mystical
complexities of poetry. Without doubt, Lanier felt that unre-
stricted inventiveness alone could liberate his deepest musical poetry.

Early in 1874 he complained that he lacked the freedom to challenge conventions; and, though he thought his poem "My Springs"
not very good, it sheds useful light on his interests in experimentation. He found that "the *forms* of today" require "trim smugness,"
and to publish at all he had to conform partially to those "tyrannies"; but he did so with a view to overturning such forms in the
future.[12] And yet the confused imagery, abstractions, allegory,
and monotonous rhythm of "My Springs" were as much rooted in
the old mannerisms of his occasional poetry as they were in the
prose-in-verse of his time. Brooks and Warren in *Understanding
Poetry* treat "My Springs" as a model of metaphorical confusion
and sentimentality.[13] Though Philip Graham has compared it to
Bryant's "O Fairest of the Rural Maids," the poem is not improved
by the connection.[14] But we must not lose perspective: Lanier
thought he was conceding to public taste and withholding the
originality that erupted in "The Symphony."

The publication of "Corn" in February, 1875, gave him a
chance to revolt against the tyrannies of conformity. His description of his intentions in "Special Pleading" on February 11 shows
his daring to give himself "some freedom in my own peculiar
style" in regard to "similes and meters." But the technical adjust-
ments Lanier made in phonetic reiteration (alliteration and assonance) and meter were not matched by improved images. As
Richard Webb has pointed out, "If the line, 'Now-time sounds so

much more fine,' is the result of freedom in versification, we pray
to be delivered from it." [15] Musical devices had been more successfully employed in "Tyranny" and "Corn."

"The Symphony" was Lanier's first controlled use of phonetic
reiteration on a large scale, and it was also his first poem to use
music imagery extensively. At first, Lanier had used it sporadically, for "Spring" (c. 1859) contains more of such images than
any poem of the next ten years. Six other early poems have picturesque musical images, two foreshadowing those of "The Symphony." "Birthday Song" (1866) contains Lanier's first flute
image.

But the first sustained use of a musical image occurs in the second poem of his sonnet cycle "In Absence" (1874–75). Striking at
the evils of intellect, the sonnet asserts a Renaissance notion of the
harmony of souls:

> So do the mottled formulas of Sense
>   Glide snakewise through our dreams of Aftertime;
> So errors breed in reeds and grasses dense
>   That bank our singing rivulets of rhyme.
> By Sense rule Space and Time; but in God's Land
>   Their intervals are not, save such as lie
> Betwixt successive tones in concords bland
>   Whose loving distance makes the harmony.
> Ah, there shall never come 'twixt me and thee
>   Gross dissonances of the mile, the year;
> But in the multichords of ecstasy
>   Our souls shall mingle, yet be featured clear,
>   And absence, wrought to intervals divine,
>   Shall part, yet link, thy nature's tone and mine.[16]

The lines linking snakelike Sense to disharmony are abrupt, for
the consonants and vowels of the second line collide—perhaps a
modification of Browning's "glottis-labyrinth" which Lanier found
useful for giving "zig-zag glimpses" of men's souls. But the harmony of "God's land" demands syzygy to facilitate movement
from one syllable to the next. Interestingly, Lanier recovers the
structure of opposition and paradoxical reconciliation that we
have seen at work in many chivalric poems: absence both parts
and joins the separate tones of the poet and his beloved.

"In Absence" shows how Lanier's musical career would sensitize him to the effects of music imagery apart from the musicality of verse, especially since "the coming reign of forgiveness and love" would produce a profound education of moral feelings. Unable to give himself to either music or poetry in 1875, Lanier imagined a cosmic unity of the two which, at the same time, would also dispel the social evil which separated sections of the country and groups of men. The very tone color and rhythm of Lanier's poetry would try to effect all of these syntheses: musical verse would etherealize poetic sentiments, and both arts would reveal the errors of reason and thus ameliorate the sources of social injustice. If "Music is Love in search of a word" states a didactic program of moral education, the music of his poem demonstrates the value of pure emotion as the sounds of the words create responses in advance of intellectual understanding, as is often the case in Walt Whitman, Algernon Swinburne, Paul Verlaine, and Dylan Thomas.

The success of "Corn" had given Lanier his first public chance to make revolutionary demonstrations of the power of feeling. Such was his "content." But style was discovered to be more important; or as Carlyle argued in his hero-poet essay, poetry is musical thought.[17] Carlyle's "See deep enough, and you see musically; the heart of Nature being everywhere music, if you can only reach it," is a thought which may have guided much nineteenth-century esthetics; for, much later George Santayana declared that all art finally aspires to the condition of music. A musical style in poetry could thus raise the verbal level and etherealize it. The content could not be entirely disowned, for Lanier was afraid his awareness of the education of feelings would be misunderstood if he relied totally on the musicality of verse. And so "The Symphony," a daring and original experiment in musical verse, is also an orchestration of many specific themes of morality, chivalry, protest and accommodation.

IV "The Symphony": Preliminary

Though odes to music and its muse had anticipated him, Lanier was the first to use the title "The Symphony." I have suggested what he meant by that title, but it is also useful to see what he did not mean. Even a cursory reading shows Lanier did not want to arrange the entire orchestra in his poem but only those instruments which symbolized "social questions of the times." Though

divisible into four "movements," the poem is not modeled on symphonic form. While the treatment of recurrent themes may suggest "symphonic" organization, no certain relation can be made
between the reiteration of themes in a poem and of those in
music. Though the themes of economic exploitation, nature, and
love are each handled by each instrument, the result is no more nor
less symphonic than in any other long poem, such as Longfellow's
Evangeline. Yet the poem ought to be distinguished from a more
conscious attempt to construct a counterpointing of themes or
symbols, as in Whitman's "When Lilacs Last in the Dooryard
Bloom'd." Lanier does not use such counterpointing; instead, he
varies the rhythm and tone color of each instrument as the themes
recur.

Lanier had summarized his intentions with a comment on
Shakespeare's line, "To hear with eyes belongs to Love's fine wit."
Writing to fellow poet Edward Spencer, he said: "In my 'Symphony,' Love's fine wit—the love of one's fellowmen—attempts
(not to hear with eyes, but precisely the reverse) to see with
ears." [18] But the process of using this metaphor as a controlling
device for the structure of a long poem was more difficult than
Lanier might have believed at the outset. Thus on March 24, 1875,
he told his wife that the poem took hold of him "Like a real James
River Ague; and I have been in a mortal shake with the same, day
and night, ever since." He told her that the instruments would
discuss "various deep social questions of the time," and he anticipated its completion since it racked "all the bones" of his spirit. [19]

V *"The Symphony": Social Consciousness*

"The Symphony" contains four sections. The first part opens as
the strings wish Trade would die, describe poverty and inhumanity, and then yield in the second and longest section to the flute's
nature song. In the third section the clarinet denounces prostitu-
tion, and the French horn praises lady worship. The poem's closing section finds the oboe urging Trade to return to innocence and
the bassoons predicting that love will return to the "modern
waste."

Even this cursory summary suggests that Lanier was using
many different kinds of organization. For example, all the ages of
man and both sexes are represented: the oboe is a boy; the flute, a
youth; the violins and clarinets, women; the French horn, a

knight; the bassoons, old men. Lanier constantly draws the sexes together in the poem as varying examples of the ubiquity of love. The love of clarinet and horn is foreshadowed at the beginning by that of the violins and "mightier Strings." Other kinds of love are asserted: the love of God, of one's neighbors, of nature, of freedom, of purity, of honor, of feeling, and of life in all its grief and joy. Trade is shown to be a disruptor of the natural relations between men, between man and nature, and between man and God by reducing men and women to objects, by debasing the poor, and by creating myths that falsify man's relation to nature.

The largest sections of the poem go to the flute, strings, and horn, following a hierarchy of value that Lanier set forth in "Retrospects and Prospects" of 1868, along with the relationship between the instruments and nature. In that essay Lanier thought that the horn represented "the dead mineral kingdom," and thus it is "the controlled and firm voice of the enduring metals." The wooden flute, which came from the vegetable kingdom, "is the pure yet passionate voice of the trees." The sinew-strung violin represents the living animal kingdom and so produces a "strange, mournful-joyful voice of blood happily bounding in veins." Thus, the kingdoms of nature have ministered to the "court of King Man." [20] In the poem, the horn is not only firm but knightly; the flute is not only passionate but lyrical; and the violins are mournful-joyful. Thus the forms and shapes of nature direct men to love. In "The Marshes of Glynn," nature performs a similar service.

Lanier's realization of the link between nature and music provided the key to etherealizing his subject, and the polarity of love and Trade had become deeply etched on his mind by this time. Early in 1874 he tersely described the "infinitely sorrowful" things he found in Baltimore and the modern "Mammon," Wheeling, West Virginia, the veritable "face of Trade" where workers were exploited and alienated from dignified, meaningful labor.[21] He had amply observed the horrors of Trade in Northern cities where he had given concerts and had consulted physicians. His letters describe the streetscapes of urban squalor, with the "forlorn faces of the starving, of the rag-people, of the criminals . . . who suffer, suffer, throughout life." [22] Lanier felt that, because of his helplessness, he could only trust that God's ways were right, though beyond man's understanding. Spiritually, Lanier felt united to the men who die "in soul and body." "The Symphony" is his symbol of that solidarity.

After abortive attempts in "Tyranny" and in "The Jacquerie" to find a symbol for the waste of human potentiality and for such repression of the soul, Lanier at last found it in Trade; and, because he had observed the Northern abuses of Trade, he was freed from charges of sectional protest. In fact, there are no traces of Southern local color in the poem. Lanier's pictures of Trade and of the poor in his letters show a sensitivity to realistic detail that contrasts with his depiction of Trade's evil in his poem. As in "Corn" and in *Tiger-Lilies*, he avoided Realism in order to pursue another style. Social correction in art often produces propaganda and thus simplicity and stereotyping—enemies of creative art. Lanier had other ideas about how society could be changed, ideas involving an ingenious manipulation of poetic images and, above all, poetic music.

Lanier had never written tracts against the disorders of his time—consider the poems inspired by the Sherman Bill and the Civil Rights Bill; instead, he examined the changes that occurred within human beings because of such laws. In "The Symphony" he was not interested in pinpointing specific social problems so that he could offer what Starke has called "an intelligible program of social amelioration"; indeed, Lanier's only "program" is the poem. Despite, therefore, Henry Steele Commager's thought that the poem is a "savage indictment of industrialism," Vernon Parrington's note that Lanier was one of the first American poets to vilify industrialism, or even John Crowe Ransom's agreement with Parrington that Lanier's protest is "incontrovertible and impressive," Lanier's reluctance to point out the specific causes or the particular men responsible for the plundering of the nation shows that he wished to examine a more general condition of injustice: the loss of love, which required a new education of feelings. And so it is the music, within the style and form of the poem, which must be understood to be Lanier's way of evaluating the human condition.

VI *"The Symphony" and the Critics*

Despite the criticism of Robert Penn Warren that Lanier was a "blind poet" who "never understood the function of idea in art" and who was, therefore, "intellectual in a bad sense" like Tennyson and the Brownings (comments to be challenged at the end of Chapter 8),[23] nevertheless Lanier's nature images in "The Symphony" are the most precise he ever wrote. His link between form and idea was far more subtle than Warren imagined, and his creation of musical effects was so subtle and ingenious that most critics have found it too elusive for their critical vocabulary. Consequently, they have largely ignored his complex use of phonetic reiteration, syzygy, rhyming, rhythm, and so forth. Starke has noted that there are too many compound words, that entire lines should have been excised, that some epithets are ridiculous, but that "The Symphony" equaled Keats, Marlowe, and Shakespeare in nature imagery.[24] Richard Webb, who tried, however, to find a relationship between the form of the poem and the instruments, notes the correlation between the themes and the "effects" of the instruments; but he gets no further than to commend the "wonderful harmony" of the poem and the striking melody of some lines.[25]

The criticism of Gay W. Allen and Charmenz Lenhart is more pertinent. In *American Prosody*, Allen examines Lanier's experiments in detail, finding that the octosyllabic couplets with anapestic substitution of the opening section attempt "to represent the rhythms and cadences of the violins";[26] but Lenhart has given the most comprehensive description of Lanier's prosody. After wishing that Lanier had used the symphonic music that he had heard in Baltimore and New York as a structure for improvisation in language (a misguided hope shared by John Gould Fletcher), Lenhart insists that Lanier used a more mechanical device "far beneath what he was capable of." She finds the themes of most of the instruments "almost laughable" and vaguely praises the flute section. Lenhart finally minimizes the poem's value by calling it "an early experiment in musico-poetic structure." [27] It was more.

VII *A Structural Analysis of "The Symphony":*
1. The Strings

The structure of the poem may be called "stichic" since there are no stanzaic divisions and, in addition, no sectional ones. But, instead of promoting diffusiveness, Lanier has carefully distinguished major and minor sections of the poem for specific effects. Edmund Stedman, summarizing the general discomfort of others who could not understand the poem's structure, called it a "mass of nebulous recitative"; but he was wrong, as a close reading shows.

The over-all sections of the poem are clearly four—given to the strings, flute, clarinet and horn, oboe and bassoon. The first section can be divided into three parts: in the first part, lines 1–12, the violins attack Trade, and a five-line "bridge" shows the entrance of the "mightier strings"; in the second part, lines 29–50, the strings first generalize about economic exploitation and imitate the voices of the poor; in the third part, lines 54–68, a four-line bridge introduces the relation between Trade and war.

The first dozen lines convincingly demonstrate a special tone color that distinguished the sound of the strings:

> "O Trade! O Trade! Would thou wert dead!
> The Time needs heart—'tis tired of head:
> We're all for love," the violins said.
> 4   "Of what avail the rigorous tale
> Of bill for coin and box for bale?
> Grant thee, O Trade! thine uttermost hope:
> Level red gold with blue sky-slope,
> 8   And base it deep as devils grope:
> When all's done, what hast thou won
> Of the only sweet that's under the sun?
> Ay, canst thou buy a single sigh
> 12   Of true love's least, least ecstasy?" [28]

These lines are tetrameter triplets with frequent substitution (mostly anapestic, as Allen has noted) and little end-stopping, giving a sense of movement toward the rhetorical questions. The monosyllabic terseness is well suited to social protest. In Paul Fussell, Jr.'s, opinion, Lanier would have benefited from end-stopping since it promotes "a symphonic sense of flow and flux, a sort of tidal variation." [29] But the iambic tetrameter worked to counteract Lanier's old tendency to diffuseness, though a prosodic form can only be an aid. According to Fussell, the tetrameter will "Circumscribe predication to its skeletal form of subject, verb, and object; it enforces a sparseness of modifiers"—and so it works in this section.

Though Lanier uses triplets mainly, he does employ couplets or groups of couplets; and in Fussell's view the couplet "is likely to be lean and clean, spare and logical . . . a texture supremely appropriate to sarcasm or solid virile reasoning." Yet triplet rhyme, a hallmark of most of the section, "tends to produce fatiguing and sometimes comic or bizarre effects." Therefore, Lanier's prosody is composed of conflicting elements, just as his intention balanced social protest against etherealized poetry. These conflicts in conception and prosody may help to explain the uneven effect of the poem, for Lanier was still in his apprenticeship and unable to follow his ideas to their logical conclusions. Of course, we could argue that the violins are not comfortable with social criticism, since they are "all for love," and that, therefore, their lines waver between the meter which is best employed for satire and criticism and the rhyme which invites lighter tones.

Within twelve lines Lanier alters the rhyme scheme from triplet to couplet twice, a characteristic aspect of the strings, as is the unusual way in which the rhyme is varied. Line four introduces a medial rhyme with the final rhyme ("avail"-"tale"); and, when the rhyme changes in line six, the rhyme word again chimes with internal words ("O"-"most"-"hope"). The same happens on nine and eleven ("done"-"won") ("buy"-"sigh"). This pattern becomes evident: when the rhyme sound changes, a word usually in the medial foot anticipates the rhyme. But Lanier varies the pattern the second or third time that the rhyme appears in order to prevent monotony. He gives unity to these dozen lines by beginning and ending with repeated words: 1: "Trade"-"Trade"; 12: "least"-"least." Both of these words are phonetically related through two families of sounds, the liquids (*r* and *l*) and the *d*-*t* group derived from the *N*-family.

Lanier uses alliteration in some striking ways to bind his most important words together and to establish the specific musicality of the violins. Lines 1 and 2 show alliterations not only on *t*s and *w*s but also on *tr* clusters from line to line, sometimes disguised ("tired") and sometimes by concealed alliteration. Kenneth Burke has proposed that sounds of the same phonetic group are related by concealed alliterations.[30] Of course, they may, if well concealed, never be felt as sound features of the poem; but they may act upon the reader unconsciously and thus let the music affect him circumspectly. Burke has also suggested the term "colliteration" for a similarity of final consonant sounds, and we notice concealed colliteration between the words tra*de* and leas*t*. But most ingeniously, Burke has demonstrated how "acrostic structures" may give "consistency with variation" by duplicating or inverting one word's sequence of sounds in another word in the same phrase; and we shall return to this interesting prosodic analysis of Burke's.

In the first two lines other sound relations besides alliterative ones are felt. In line 1, "Would thou wert dead" sounds effective because the *d-t-d-* colliterate and the *th-d* alliterate. In line 2, the same key sounds are used: in "The Time needs heart—'tis tired of head" the *n* takes its place in the concealed alliteration, while the aspirated *h* in the medial foot (heart) works with the *h* of "head" to produce a sense of strain and urgency. Returning to Burke's acrostic structures, the *tr-d* of "Trade" is changed to *r-t-d* of "wert dead"; and also *r-t-t-* of "heart—'tis." The original pattern is reinstated in "tired" with t-r-d. As for the last couplet, lines 11–12, the alliteration of *s* in 11 and *l* in 12 is apparent. But the chief sound of line 3 is *r-l*, a liquid sound suited to love as the congested cluster "*trd*" and its variations are suitable to war. In line 11, Lanier uses *st* (can*st*) which is repeated with variation in "lea*st*, lea*st*, ec*st*asy." The proliferation of this kind of tone color in these twelve lines creates a sound recognized as belonging to the strings, but the recognition may not be a very conscious one.

The "bridge" which follows creates a different kind of music. At least four of the five lines are trochaic in the first foot, in strong contrast to the predominant iambic first feet of lines 1–12, though lines 6, 7, and 9 contain trochaic first feet:

13   Then, with a bridegroom's heart-beats trembling,
        All the mightier strings assembling
        Ranged them on the violins' side
        As when the bridegroom leads the bride,
17   And, heart in voice, together cried:

The violins told Trade it could not purchase love (as it would try to do again in the third section of the clarinet) and the arrival of strings as bridegrooms chivalricly defends them. In line 17, as the strings prepare to speak to the violins, the lines becomes iambic tetrameter, smoothly blending to the violins' meter. But in giving the strings a distinctive voice, Lanier uses double feminine rhymes. If the iambic rhythm of the violins was "rising," the rhythm of lines 13–14 is surely "falling." While the violins used occasional anapestic substitutions (lines 3, 4, 6, and 10) the feet of the violins are now changed to dactyllic (line 13). And, as the violins end at line 12, a rare spondee is inserted as a substituted third foot, preparing for the shifting of the stress to the initial part of the foot in the bridge. Clearly, Lanier was developing a rich orchestration of sound of intensity and variety.

The second part of the string section opens with an echo of the violins' fourth line, as if picking up a theme for development presented in the "introduction" section of this "movement."

18   "Yea, what avail the endless tale
             Of gain by cunning and plus by sale?
             Look up the land, look down the land—
             The poor, the poor, the poor, they stand
             Wedged by the pressing of Trade's hand
             Against an inward-opening door
24   That pressure tightens evermore:
             They sigh a monstrous foul-air sigh
             For the outside leagues of liberty,
             Where Art, sweet lark, translates the sky
28   Into a heavenly melody.[31]

The repetition re-establishes the pattern of assonance anticipation, for the first and second rhymes have internal rhyme the first time they appear. Though the third rhyme does not, the fourth returns to the pattern with the repeated word "sigh." Alliteration is minimal; assonance, unimportant; consonance, nonexistent. But the repeated words are the new tone color which the violins developed to accompany the new themes, or the developed themes.

The strings' imitations of the poor folks' protest brings in another kind of sound duplication:

29   'Each day, all day' (these poor folks say),
             'In the same old year-long, drear-long way,
             We weave in the mills and heave in the kilns,
             We sieve mine-meshes under the hills,
             And thieve much gold from the Devil's bank tills,
             To relieve, O God, what manner of ills?'

Aside from word repetitions, line 30 contains the first incidence of double internal rhyme. And it creates a perpendicular rhyme: "weave"-"thieve"-"relieve" (with a sight rhyme possibly on "sieve"). Following the plea of the poor, Lanier drops his sound devices one by one, altering the rhyme pattern and meter instead. Lines 35–40 rhyme six consecutive lines, and lines 40–47 shift rhyme only slightly from "tone"-"alone"-"Throne" to "so"-"No"-"know"-"Go." Lines 44 and 45 have two feet, and the striking line "Trade is trade," line 50, is headless and is echoed in form later in the flute section and inverted in the clarinet-horn section.

The four-line bridge that follows repeats the double feminine rhymes, but on alternate lines. The last two of the bridge shift from four to three feet and suggest the change in the strings' tone by heavy assonances and alliterations, as well as acrostic alliteration on s-$t(d)$ and interlinear rhyme:

53   It sank to sad requesting
                    And suggesting sadder still:

The closing part of the violin section uses devices from all previous parts but expands the internal rhymes:

58   Does business mean, *Die, you—live, I?*
            Then 'Trade is trade' but sings a lie:
            'Tis only war grown miserly.
61   If business is battle, name it so:
            War-crimes less will shame it so,
            And widows less will blame it so.
            Alas: for the poor to have some part
            In yon sweet living lands of Art,
66   Makes problem not for head, but heart.
            Vainly might Plato's brain revolve it:
            Plainly the heart of a child could solve it."

The most striking feature of these lines is the five-word rhyme of lines 62–63. It brings the use of feminine rhyme in the poem to its peak and marks the first time the rhyme word for two or more lines is the same. The result is chantlike, and it is intensified by the closing couplet which begins and ends with feminine double rhymes.

Unquestionably, the poem is a tour de force of the musicality of verse. Though we are tempted to do so it is not necessary to follow in detail the music in the next three sections to indicate the way Lanier establishes the voices of the other instruments. We ought to recall our purpose, however, before proceeding, to show how Lanier's interest in the musicality of verse arose from a determination to educate the feelings of his age. This analysis of only 20 percent of the poem shows that Lanier had found unending possibilities for etherealizing poetry, though we might decide, of course, that he neglected to let the sound echo to the sense; but I think additional study of the poem reveals otherwise.

VIII   *"The Symphony"*: 2. *The Flute*

The strings have assailed Trade as intellectual, blasphemous, warmongering, hypocritical, tyrannical, inhumane, and philistine —exactly the same charges implied in Lanier's letter of 1860 and described in the characters of John Cranston in *Tiger-Lilies* and Lord Raoul in "The Jacquerie." And he now pursues the same pattern exhibited in the letter, his fiction, and his poetry: reconciliation and regeneration. While it is too early in the poem for conclusive notes of redemption to sound, the violins section closes on a note foreshadowing affirmation, for, after a long bridge marked by a use of feminine double rhyme, Lanier compares the sobbing strings to a "sleeping bird," a bird which at the poem's end brings love to the wasteland. The flute enters with a different meter, iambic pentameter, the one most closely related to actual speech intonation in English. The introductory image is unfortunately grotesque though sonically interesting:

96   Somewhat, half song, half odor, forth did float,
            As if a rose might somehow be a throat:

Line 96 alliterates and colliterates *f*, but the "tonal chiasmus" (to use another of Burke's terms) reverses the order of vowels. The first four syllables make a pattern of mirrored sounds: *o-a-a-o*. The group of vowels in "odor, forth did float" moves from *o-or* to *or-o*. Lanier does not merely juggle words and sounds since the next line has no perceivable chiasmus, and thus Lanier seems to have intended to use back-vowels and clusters of fricatives and liquids to approximate the flute's "rose throat." The smooth blank verse may assist this effect.

Like the "corn-captain," the flute comes directly from nature and speaks for "all-shaped blooms and leaves,/Lichens on stones and moss on eaves." Lanier's meter now shifts to irregular tetra-

meter with lines 162 and 163, substituting spondees and pyrrhics
to emphasize the wonder of the flute's range:

> Vale-calms and tranquil lotos-sleeps;—
> 162   Yea, all fair forms, and sounds, and lights,
> And warmths, and mysteries, and mights,
> Of Nature's utmost depths and heights,

The frequent caesuras and end-stopping prompt a musical phras-
ing, while the alliterative and colliterative liquids and the acrostic
structuring of the *N* group of consonant sounds are blended to the
predominant back-vowels of "calms," "lotos," and "all." Together
they give a darker color to the flute's second section.

Some of the finest imagery and most musical phrases Lanier
ever created are in the flute's section. Near "pistils, and petals
crystalline," fly "film-winged things." The Jay "hints tragedies"
with "sparklings of small beady eyes." When merged to sound
devices, the lines reach a summit of Lanier's power:

> 153   Each dial-marked leaf and flower-bell
> Wherewith in every lonesome dell
> Time to himself his hours doth tell;
> 156   All tree-sounds, rustlings of pine-cones,
> Wind-sighings, doves' melodious moans,
> 158   And night's unearthly under-tones:

This passage shows unobtrusive but effective weavings of the *M*
group (*m-n-p-b-f-v*) and the *N* group. The diction is specific and
the rhyme words chosen to link together words of the sounds of
nature. The phrase "doves' melodious moans" recalls Tennyson's
famous "murmuring of innumerable bees" in its onomatopoeia.

The flute section is the longest and the most seductive, but it
creates doubt about its organic function in the poem. For the first
theme sounded in the poem was social injustice, and the flute has
withdrawn into nature; but, ironically, instead of discovering
Transcendental insights, it recovers the theme of the violins. The
flute first explores Lanier's notion that man at last is a brother to
nature, using the violins' "All for love" as a point of departure.
This idea of the etherealized relation of nature to man leads asso-
ciatively to the theme of man's inhumanity to man. With form

following sense, the iambic pentameter of the etherealization passage dissolves and is replaced by a loosened iambic tetrameter which repeats with variations lines 21–28:

191   But oh, the poor! the poor! the poor!
      That stand by the inward-opening door
      Trade's hand doth tighten ever more,
      And sigh their monstrous foul-air sigh
195   For the outside hills of liberty,
      Where Nature spreads her wild blue sky
      For Art to make into melody!

By imitating the music as well as the images of the violins, Lanier binds the flute section to the strings section and shows that withdrawal into nature is only a brief respite for future battles with the enemy. The flute's final lines echo the opening theme of the strings and its "coda":

205   Trade! is thy heart all dead, all dead?
      And hast thou nothing but a head?
      I'm all for heart," the flute-voice said.

After opening with a variation in the usual meter of the poem, altering the length of feet from one to five feet, rhyming uneven feet, and using phrases to suggest rhythmic groupings, the flute has returned to the rhythmic starting point and disappeared. Lanier was now faced with the problem of sustaining the reader's interest without becoming mannered or boring, and a partial solution was to repeat the scheme of the first two movements with the variety offered by duos of instruments, rather than single voices. And thus he could make smaller divisions of his last two "movements" and partly overcome the disadvantages of the large form he had chosen. The clarinet-horn section has tighter metrical forms and includes a ballad. The last section of oboe and bassoon is freer in line variation and tone color than any of the others.

IX *"The Symphony": 3. Clarinet and Horn*

In this section Lanier uses alliteration and vowel chiasmus to accentuate through cacophony the horror of the misuse of women. Reiterating the theme of the violins, the clarinet also wishes Trade

would die because of the "shameful ways" of women "At the
beckoning of Trade's golden rod!" Such exploitation will naturally
move to destroy nature next:

225   Alas when sighs are traders' lies,
              And heart's-ease eyes and violet eyes
              Are merchandise!

The unfortunate preciosity of these lines is offset by the atypical
congestion of assonances and consonances, making rapid movements from back vowels (*heart's*) to front vowels (*ease*) then to a
back glide (*eyes*), and accompanying movements from a voice-
less dental (*heart*) to a series of voiced *s*'s. The result is a contrived phonetic log jam, a Browningesque dissonance to under-
score the outrage of the abused lady.

In section one, the bridegroom strings came quickly to the violins' aid; now the French horn defends the clarinet from Trade.
Lanier had claimed in "The Orchestra of Today" that no one
could fail to detect the "peculiarly feminine character" of the clarinet's higher registers and, riding out of "The Jacquerie," the
French horn responds to the clarinet by fitting its strength of
character to the strongest form in the poem, the ballad, in thirteen
stanzas rhyming *aaa4a3B1*, ending with a refrain "Fair lady," an
amphibrach. Chivalry lives, despite Lord Raoul, and the decadant
institution is transformed. The horn, like the "mightier strings"
opposes Trade with a Christian manliness.

To individualize the horn's voice, Lanier develops an interesting rhyme scheme to go with his ballad. He varies the rhyme from
stanza to stanza only slightly, thus linking the ideas of the stanzas
tightly together and reinforcing the solidity of the horn's voice.
Since the first stanza rhymes "morn-scorn," the second "wrong-
song," the fourth "grave-knave" and the fifth "slain-gain," the thirteen stanzas can be grouped in threes, for two stanzas use similar
rhyme words, but the third stanza of the group changes to a very
different sound. There are minor variations for variety.

The horn pledges his undying chivalry while fighting in the "patient modern way" (poetry and song?), but it is never clear how
love can be asserted in an unjust world or why the horn imagines
his "modern way" can contend with modern Trade. In terms of

the immediate context, Lanier very likely wants to suggest that, without lady worship, the exploitation of women is inevitable. Apparently the horn vanquishes his foe through his music, having etherealized Trade, for spiritualization is in fact the modern way. Lanier has acted out his notion that, in the cyclic nature of things, Chivalry must rise to overthrow Trade through the leadership of a great man.

X *"The Symphony": 4. Oboe and Bassoon*

Continuing the chivalric mood, Lanier calls the oboe a "hautboy," but the fourth section is a step further back in time than Camelot: the child as hautboy is a concretion of the violins' assertion that only a child could resolve social injustice. Picking up the theme of the strings, flute, and horn, the oboe echoes Christ:

333   *Never shalt thou the heavens see,*
               Save as a little child thou be."

The substituted trochees in the initial foot make the pronouncement dramatic, and the simple biblical words emphasize how wise a child he is. The oboe wishes to sit on the head of Trade (to elevate his heart above it?) and direct it—as usual Lanier condemns the *misuse* of Trade and intellect, not their *existence*. The child's simple remarks give a serious turn to the argument against Trade which no commentators have found important, but which in fact is the source for understanding the democratic poems of 1876. This simple theme is unadorned by complex prosody or tone color.

By now it is clear that the "great man" who appeared as the "corn-captain" has appeared in the disguise of all the instruments of "The Symphony." In the third section, he emerges as a knight, but he now takes the form of the prophet, personified by the bassoon. The bassoons' paradoxical images create a mystical vision of "the coming reign of beauty and art." While Lanier had found the oboe "peculiarly simple, child-like," he found the bassoon capable of a "very remarkable combination of gravity and sensuous richness." Since love unites opposites, it is fitting that the bassoon opens with descriptions of contrasts in the image of the pulsating sea:

341   "Bright-waved gain, gray waved loss,
                      The sea of all doth lash and toss,
                      One wave forward and one across:
                      But now 'twas trough, now 'tis crest,
                      And worst doth foam and flash to best,
                          And curst to blest.

The bassoons' entrance is odd, for we sense that its rhythm is
based on a stress or time system, rather than on a stress-syllable
count, as Lanier outlined it later in *The Science of English Verse.*
The first foot of line 341 may be a dactyl or a spondee; line 344
has an extra foot. Though he has not abandoned the syllable system, Lanier seems to give the feeling of syllablic verse emerging
from a different type, one which works with time in a different
way and may antedate it. Perhaps he is suggesting that this older
procedure is in reality the poetry of the future, becoming, as he
argued in many essays, more like prose as it loses the bonds of
formal meter. Whatever the reason, the flux contributed to the
verse effectively gives the motion of the sea; and the acrostic alliteration with augmentation and inversion accompany the flux of
the rhythm rather well. In "twas trough, now 'tis crest" *t-s* and
t-r of " 'twas trough" combine in *r-s-t* of "crest." Line 345 shows
a striking use of concealed alliteration on the *M* and *N* groups,
as well as colliteration. These various devices seem to summarize
all the music of the previous instruments in a grand imitation by
the bassoon.

The sea's spin-drift moods have prepared for the musical metaphor which leads directly to the mystical vision:

347   "Life Life! thou sea-fugue, writ from east to west,
                     Love, Love alone can pore
                     On thy dissolving score
                     Of harsh half-phrasings,
                         Blotted ere writ,
                     And double erasings
                         Of chords most fit.
                     Yea, Love, sole music-master blest,
                     May read thy weltering palimpsest.
                     To follow Time's dying melodies through,
                     And never to lose the old in the new,
                     And ever to solve the discords true—
                         Love alone can do.

The meter now fluctuates rapidly, varying the phrasings and fitting music to sense as conflicting discords match resolving chords. Love supplies the other half of the "harsh half-phrasings" to create a tonic chord. And Love is the main theme of the orchestra because it unifies the many voices and styles of the instruments; they are literally "all for love." Love unites the old and new, and it reads through a vertical view of life the core of tensions that have always characterized the human condition. What had begun in social protest now ends by describing the spiritual discord and the spiritual wasteland created by "Reconstructed" but unregenerate men.

The bassoon has used the feminine double rhymes of the "bridges," the varied meter of the flute, and the alliterative and assonantal devices of the strings. Now it uses the chant of the violins:

360   And ever Love hears the poor-folks' crying,
           And ever Love hears the women's sighing,
           And ever sweet knighthood's death-defying,
           And ever wise childhood's deep implying,
364   But never a trader's glozing and lying.

It may be a surprise that the "ancient wise bassoons" are the ones to proclaim the meaning of Love, but in Lanier's 1860 letter he had insisted that "harmony," by which, we remember, he meant the supremacy of feeling, would be obvious even to ancient people without the Bible or modern metaphysics. The many participle rhymes hint that the spiritual descent is at hand.

Since love had been unable to hear Trade, perhaps because this musical tribute, Lanier's "Symphony," had overcome its dissonance, one guesses that Trade simply and spontaneously etherealizes in its presence. The poem could end here, but the bassoons provide an epilogue that is a coda to the symphony and the poem:

365   "And yet shall Love himself be heard,
           Though long deferred, though long deferred:
           O'er the modern waste a dove hath whirred:
           Music is Love in search of a word."

The lower case *h* of "himself" does not distract us from recognizing the advent of Christ and the Second Coming. The instruments have made all varieties of love their theme; and Love himself, the Great man, has responded. In Lanier's poem, as in his metaphysics, not only is God Love, but Love is God.

Lanier had often used the dove as a bird of prophecy. It appears frequently in 1875 and was used in eight other poems, some of which have been noted. All the other birds—ravens, pigeons, falcons, jays, mudhens, larks—in some ways share the spiritual connotations of the dove. But only the dove has the most important religious meanings: peace (Genesis 8:8–12); gentleness (Matthew 10:16); and the Holy Ghost (Leviticus 14:22). As Noah's dove sought land and found it through God's mercy, so does the religious word that man accepts on faith become concretized in an image of a rainbow. For Lanier, the image is that of the dove; for, like the rainbow, the dove assures Lanier that the modern waste will not destroy itself. The dove is, therefore, a sign that the theme of "The Symphony" will be realized, giving purpose and rationale to Lanier's complex esthetic procedures in creating a musical verse. The dove's spiritual voice is also proof that music is "a whole great step nearer the infinite." Perhaps to suggest the perfect relation between the ear, the flight of the dove, and the Word of God, Lanier has made the perfect rhymes "heard-whirred-bird."

Lanier had written in "Retrospects and Prospects" that music's "two dove's-wings" would carry "a whole world-full of people to Heaven!" [32] In "The Symphony," he had demonstrated the morality of feeling through the interaction of musical instruments and God's instrument; through the manipulation of music metaphors; and, above all, through the employment of a rich musical poetry. The error of the age had deafened man to his own intuitive recognition of the place of love in his life, but future poetry exemplified by this poem, would restore the proper sense of true spiritual harmony. In recovering man's capacity to love, Lanier had found his poetic voice.

XI   *Aftermath*

The poem's length, didacticism, sentimentality, and repetitiousness were the weaknesses of a young poet supremely sensitive to the sonic possibilities of language but never a good self-critic.

Nevertheless, his determined pursuit of the sound of poetry did not hinder his concern for its sense, though it seems to have often allowed him to choose words for their tone color rather than for their perfect applicability or function. But Lanier seems to have found the best method by which to buttress his desire to educate feelings, for the music subtly affects the reader even against his will, though the images and ideas may be resisted intellectually. As was customary with Lanier, once he had satisfied himself with an experiment, he took a different direction; and his subsequent career suggests that he saw the limitation of this method in "The Symphony" and tried thereafter to capitalize upon the theme of the growth of soul to control his images and his music.

Meanwhile, Lanier was educating himself to be a professional musician, and he even made the surprising admission in 1875 that, though he expressed himself with "most freedom" in poetry, his "present stage of growth" was more passionately devoted to music: "I am not its master, it is mine." [33] He tried to redirect his musical interests toward poetry when he wrote *The Science of English Verse*, but he ran the risk of subordinating everything to music and thus to the charge that his poetry was an elaborate rationalization of his practices. As Kenneth Burke has said, the more a poet arrives at an "explicit formulation of his tactic," the more he is led to a "more efficient exploitation of the method, so that his manner threatens to degenerate into a mannerism." Such was the path of Swinburne, Gerard Manley Hopkins, and some of the French Symbolists; but we can hardly blame Lanier or other nineteenth-century poets if they took such a direction. For, as John Crowe Ransom has said, an American poet of 1875 could hardly be expected to know what intelligent modern poets know because the modern poet has access to a vast experimentation and a vast body of criticism.[34]

To Bayard Taylor, "The Symphony" announced a "new right-fully anointed poet," with an "unusual instinct of rhythm." [35] Lanier had at last taken part in a modern movement in poetry and had at last joined the avant-garde. In 1875, he assumed that, if his latest poetry were not successful, the cause lay in its "perfect newness . . . absolute unlikeness." He never worried that the new might not be true, and he made, therefore, some poetical blunders before finding a true link between his major themes and his artistic talents.

He never tired reminding his wife what his major theme was, for he wrote in 1875: "As Christ gathered up the ten commandments and re-distilled them into the clear liquid of that wondrous eleventh—Love God utterly, and thy neighbor as thyself—so I think the time will come when music, rightly developed to its now-little-foreseen grandeur, will be found to be a later revelation of all gospels in one." [36] Since music was synonymous with feeling, the pure distillate of music containing all gospels in one is pure feeling. Lanier could never mention the problems of his epoch without at once seeing the cure. In his "Marsh" poems, Lanier dramatized the etherealizing power of nature through images of Transcendental conversion, charged by a subjectivism created by his musical verse. He learned slowly, but he learned well.

CHAPTER 6

The Poetry of Freedom

"THE Symphony" had orchestrated Lanier's major themes, but such a synthesis evaded him when he tried to become a spokesman for public morality in "The Centennial Cantata" and in "The Psalm of the West," which were commissioned on the strength of "The Symphony." Though Lanier was always in some ways optimistic about the eventual triumph of the democratic spirit, these poems fail because of the obvious strain to promote democracy comprehensively and completely. Between the writing of these poems in 1876 and the completion of "The Marshes of Glynn" in 1878, Lanier's poetry changed decisively toward a deepening exploration of subjective states. But he first blundered into the trap Burke warned against and made a mannerism of his musicality of verse. In addition, he unrestrainedly relied upon diffuse imagery without the re-enforcement of symbolic imagination.

Lanier's later career seems so marked by such a scattering of his resources that he appears erratic and confused as he "proves" Shakespeare inferior to George Eliot, becomes absorbed in Anglo-Saxon writing, and edits medieval romances for boys. Yet all his interests from *The Science of English Verse* to "How to Read Chaucer" attest to the power of the "moral sentiments" tradition in which he early placed himself. No matter what sidetracks diverted him, he followed an almost instinctive path toward his finest poetry.

I *"The Centennial Meditation"*

On December 28, 1875, Bayard Taylor told Lanier that the Philadelphia Centennial Commission wanted Lanier to write a cantata to be sung at the opening ceremonies, noting that he should "keep down the play of fancy (except where it may give room for a fine musical phrase)" and express general rather than

individual ideas of the nation.[1] As usual, Lanier followed his intuition, but he underrated the difficulties of writing singable lines
of poetry. Though he told Dudley Buck, the composer, that he
wrote poetry with "broad bands of color" and that the various
sections of his poem easily lent themselves to program music, he
did not warn Buck of the problems that he encountered which
later demanded explanation.

Lanier recognized that only the most sharply contrasting moods
or "ideas" could be used in music, and so it was natural that,
within the sixty-line poem, he should use vivid oppositions of tone,
meter, and diction. The first stanza shows a "colossal figure in
meditation"; and it has, therefore, regular rhythm and monosyllabic words. The "Mayflower" stanza has suggestions of "agitated
sea movement"—Lanier's side note—in its rhythms, and in the
"Jamestown" stanza, Lanier mirrored the bitter cold winter by a
"cold and ghostly tone-color" achieved through "long e vocables in
order to bring out a certain bassoon quality of tone from the human voices." [2]

Through a mistake, Lanier's poem was published before being
performed with the music, and the poem created a storm of protest. The usually hostile *Nation* called it "a communication from
the spirit of Nat Lee, rendered through a Bedlamite medium."
But the *Baltimore Bulletin* said that "such poetry must lie on the
borderland between thought and melody . . . its artistic treatment is original and striking." In April, Bayard Taylor at Lanier's
request, defended the poem, and Lanier wrote a lengthy analysis
after its performance on May 10, 1876, at the Centennial Exposition.

Such controversy is surprising, for the poem's allegory is conventional, its hundred-year backward glance contains inoffensive
images, and its themes and structure are simple. But Lanier's extensive use of quotations within declamations and of compound
words created problems for Buck, as did these following lines,
which Lanier ordered to be sung as a "rapid and intense whisper-
chorus":

> Toil through the stertorous death of the Night,
> Toil when wild brother-wars new-dark the Light,

Nearly impossible to sing, the lines draw Lanier's ear into question; when Buck courteously protested, Lanier exerted profes-

sional rank: "it is a maxim among poets to vary the vowel-sounds as much as possible in every line." [3] Lanier evoked this Keatsian idea when he was in difficulty, but he did not follow it consistently—a good example of how Lanier had moved toward mannerism.

The major problems of metaphors and music are found in the final stanza when the "Good Angel" promises that America will prosper as "Long as Art shall love true love," and the full chorus greets music's reign. In his first draft, Lanier wrote:

> Then, Music, from this height be thou my voice:
> In thy large tongue all tongues of earth rejoice: [4]

The dove of "The Symphony," which sought in music a language of love, has settled upon the modern world; therefore, the prophecy of that poem has been fulfilled in "The Centennial Cantata." Later Lanier perfected the tone color but obscured the meaning of this passage:

> O Music, from this height of time my Word unfold:
> In thy large signals all men's hearts Man's Heart behold:

Buck at once protested that the longer lines "compel shorter values in notation within one & the same measure, & work against what you desire." Lanier must have been stung to agreement about the odd tone color, and perhaps Buck's remarks inspired him to think about using musical notation to indicate poetic rhythm, an idea he explored in essays written during 1877–78, published as *The Science of English Verse*.

II *"The Psalm of the West"*

Lanier's convoluted praise of music at the conclusion of the cantata may appear more genuine if the following record of his interior tensions be considered. Before the attacks from the *Nation,* Lanier wrote to his wife:

> The times are out of joint:—and I seem to hear a certain voice from far off (within) calling me to set them right . . . I hear myself asking myself across a noise like that of crackling flames and

falling timbers whether the mild ministry of poetry and of music which I love is the only work I am entitled to do or commissioned to do, a fierce sense of spiritual battle against the sins of the Church and the state blares like a trumpet in my heart,—and then I awake, exhausted and trembling, and am ill with pure weakness for days.[5]

Lanier could never give up poetry, however; and he knew that to put his times right he had to put his trust in synthesizing the two arts. Unlike Hamlet—to Lanier, a symbol of the nineteenth century because of his irresolute doubt—Lanier offered himself as the great man "with the proud if pained heart of the reformer, to spend himself in bettering the state of his fellows." A poetic protest like "The Symphony" or a murky musical "Centennial Cantata" were both in their separate ways dead ends. A new direction was needed, but Lanier was also himself "out of joint" for the moment.

Ironically, the poem won Lanier the title of "the representative of the South in American Song" (in Taylor's influential phrase), though he felt repelled by the "tobacco-sodden bosh" of critical Southern editors and was trying to cut his sectional ties to win acceptance in the cultural avant-garde. Yet Lanier could produce good poetry again only after he had returned to the South in spirit. However, because of his momentary publicity, he accepted a commission to write "The Psalm of the West," whose idealized portrait of the nation suggests the moral ideal for his era.

In his mind the poem was linked to music by its very form. In *Shakespeare and His Forerunners,* he wrote that "psalm" comes from a Greek word meaning *"to play on a musical instrument."* [6] This may explain why he attempted to convert the poem into a "Choral Symphony" at the end of his life. Many of his practices in "The Psalm of the West" resemble those of "The Symphony," with forms like the sonnet and ballad enclosed within the poem; variations in tone color, in rhymes, and in phonetic reiteration; and the familiar incantatory repetitions, especially in the stanza in which the contradictory forces of art and science, the individual and the "All," are unified by love.[7]

To counter pessimism about the new land, Lanier figures the East and West as wings of a lark, recalling again his religious aviary; but he extends the image and strains it by trying to make point-for-point allegorical connections between reality and his metaphor ("One wing was feathered with facts of the uttermost Past"). Again, the length of such lines reflect the breadth of the subject but were better suited to the sweeping lines of "The Marshes of Glynn" and "Sunrise." Reaching back to "Corn" and "The Jacquerie," Lanier tries to give some depth to his lark symbol; but those who know his work recognize his self-imitation, and those who do not would be as mystified as Howells was with "Corn," and for a better reason.

Weak though it may be, the lark symbol shows that, although Lanier had returned to the various faults exemplified in his occasional poetry, he had also returned to the theme which had been important in his work shortly after the war—freedom. The lark as a symbol of freedom is given the stature of a persona, like the corn-captain, as the poem continues and as God grants it a view of past times.

In seven sonnets Lanier describes the voyage of Columbus, choosing to view him as a Carlylean hero rather than an Emersonian one. Matching form to theme, Lanier uses the freer Petrarchan rather than Shakespearean or Spenserian sonnet form, while maintaining the same form in the octave of each, though he varies the sestet. Thus the sonnets suggest Columbus himself through their form of freedom matched to resoluteness. But Lanier does not explore the special problems of his form—the unbalance of octave and sestet, the use of the "turn" in the ninth line, the function of the envelope rhymes in the two quatrains. Here again is proof that Lanier was uncomfortable with strophic forms.

Curiously, Lanier reuses a segment of "The Joust Betwixt Heart and Brain" for a segment about the Civil War, a ridiculous stratagem in the context of a "psalm" of the West, despite his modest alterations. This final borrowing from his previous work signals beyond doubt that Lanier did not have his heart in "The Psalm of the West." Although he may have easily convinced himself that he could praise a nation which only a few years before had prompted atypical protest poetry from his pen, his deeper creative resources were not stirred.

Perhaps Lanier thought the use of the Heart-Brain allegory a covert attack on the North (quite unlikely), or maybe it shows a real change since 1865. His motives were obscure, but the effect is certain. Though John Crowe Ransom feels that the opposition was "anticipatory rather than descriptive" of the true feelings between North and South, for "Brain had filled the interval with humiliations for Heart; and Heart had been very surly," [8] such serious thoughts are rendered pointless by the last stanza:

> Heart and Brain! no more be twain;
> Throb and think, one flesh again!
> Lo! they weep, they turn, they run;
> Lo! they kiss: Love, thou art one!

Unwittingly, Lanier made the most serious part of the poem almost comic. His attempts at a nationalistic etherealization, a successful occasional poem, and a national reputation as spokesman for public morality all failed. But, as always, Lanier's failures are informative; and those of "The Psalm of the West" show that his personal poetic voice, acquired with so much difficulty, could not function in the larger context of his national community. As Pearce effectively argues, Lanier may have been led deeper into his subjective, Transcendental poetry because of this.[9] As I have tried to show, Lanier's intuitive direction was always inward, but he lacked the self-critical ability and the time in which to develop the enormous confidence needed to become a complete Symbolist poet.

Lanier's pursuit of a national voice also led him to some questionable optimisms. As Robert Penn Warren has forcefully noted, Lanier failed to see "that the nationalism mystically embodied in the *Psalm of the West* was a nationalism of Trade. Amor vincit omnia—even the contradiction." [10] Allen Tate suggests that Lanier was starkly pragmatic in fawning to the North, despite his legitimate feeling shown in "The Symphony"; in other words, Lanier seemingly took Taylor's advice seriously and suppressed his individual feeling for national praise. These things render unacceptable Frederick Conner's thought that Lanier wrote as a "son of his age" in making a "paean of American greatness." [11] Nor should we too readily accept Tate's sharp assertion that "The Psalm of the West" is a "praise of 'nationalism,' *argal* of Northern sectionalism, *argal* of industrialism." However, Tate has accounted well for Lanier's strange affirmation so soon after a poem of social protest: "He believed . . . he must defer to public taste, consciously, in order the better at some time later to instruct it. No one who has

studied his career will deny that he did both; though one must
admit that his instruction could have been better than it was." [12]
Tate begs several questions. Does deferring to public taste automatically impair poetry? Would Lanier's "instruction" have been
better by not deferring to public taste? What was the relation
between Lanier's art and his instruction? Some answers to these
questions have already been presented in previous analyses of
Lanier's poems, but further specific analysis of his poetry will clarify our conclusions.

III   *The Idea of Freedom and the New Poetry*

"The Psalm of the West" is Lanier's most extensive tribute to
freedom, though not so effective as his embodiment of the subject
in the "Marsh" poems. The symbol must have originated in his
early religious recognition that man can only choose goodness if
he is free. Etherealization blended rather well to this theory, for
all things—physical, esthetic, or abstract—were free to discard
their finite structures in order to discover their "ideal selves." As
music grew more etherealized when it freed itself from the song
form which had bound it to poetry, so poetry could grow freer by
imitating music through rhyme, rhythm, and tone color. The
theory allowed Lanier the moral rationalization he needed to experiment with poetry, for he condemned "art for art's sake" as an
excuse for moral laxity.

But Lanier was troubled by some of his conclusions. For, if poetry freed itself by stripping away traditional approaches to technique, then the etherealized poetry might necessarily be simpler
in form. However, Lanier believed that what was modern was
also more complex, more comprehensive, and more spiritual.
Thus, in his lectures on Shakespeare and on the English novel, he
decided that true freedom meant the inclusion of forms rather
than their deletion. And so Lanier was led to the odd conclusion
that prose is more complex than poetry. But he knew that spiritual
freedom lay in a continuous synthesizing of experiences and that
this kind of freedom characterized the greatest artists of any art.
He made a facile extension of this argument to include the development of music, science, personality, and literary genres. Many
of these ideas are in "The Psalm of the West," showing the poem
to be a "closure" of Lanier's important ideas; but his ideas are
made less effective by his mishandling of poetic techniques.

As usual, Lanier followed his inner gleam, and when the poem
was rejected, he insisted in 1876 that it was in fact the start of a
whole new mode of poetry: "it is new, and as of old so now there
is much stoning of the prophets who preach new Gospels." [13] If the
people were badly in need of the "gospel" of music, they needed
no less the evangel of poetry. The tenacity with which Lanier held
to his confident belief that he had originated a new poetry is dis-
closed in his somber, eloquent, and faintly self-pitying rejection of
the rejectors of "The Centennial Meditation":

> What possible claim can contemporary criticism set up to respect
> —that contemporary criticism which crucified Jesus Christ, stoned
> Stephen, hooted Paul for a madman, tried Luther for a criminal,
> tortured Galileo, bound Columbus in chains, drove Dante into
> a hell of exile, made Shakespeare write the Sonnet "when in dis-
> grace with fortune and men's eyes &c.", gave Milton five pounds
> for Paradise Lost, kept Samuel Johnson cooling his heels on Lord
> Chesterfield's door-step, reviled Shelley as an unclean dog, killed
> Keats, cracked jokes on Gluck, Schubert, Beethoven, Berlioz and
> Wagner, and committed so many other impious follies and stupidi-
> ties that a thousand letters like this could not suffice even to cata-
> logue them? [14]

Lanier's marshaling of mighty associations had fortified his resolution to educate the feelings of his age, assuring him of the
greatest freedom with which to carry out his program of education. He thought his place in history assured, for the cantata
would "come to take its place as a pioneer poem in a School
whose very fundamental principles have not yet been dreamed of
by any English writer besides myself." [15] This large claim is
matched by his thought that "The Psalm of the West" could offer
a text "to preach from." Lanier had found that the "joy of human
helpfulness" that he experienced in aiding younger poets was
added to "the intrinsic delight of prophet-hood." If the coming
generation of new poets profited from his mistreatment, he would
be amply rewarded, for they could bring about the inevitable spiritualization of the nineteenth century. "I do not hate the people,"
he wrote in 1876, "who have so cruelly maltreated me; they know
not what they did: and my life will be of some avail if it shall
teach even one of them a consideration that may bloom in ten-
derer treatment of any future young artist." [16]

"The Song of the Chattahoochee," though unequal to Lanier's Christ-like pose, was a new and special blending of music and poetry in the service of a freedom which obeyed a higher morality. And, though this new independence Lanier had carefully created for himself ultimately produced "The Marshes of Glynn," it is certainly unfortunate that he did not break entirely from the attempt to write for his community and produce a fuller curriculum of poems for that new "School" he had started. But, so long as he desired to educate the feelings of his community, he could not entirely make that final rupture with it. The dream of founding a new "School" of poetry might have been attractive esthetically, psychologically, and socially; but it was impossible, for he had long ago dedicated himself to another dream of higher priority which he had followed with perfect obedience.

The inclusion of "The Centennial Meditation" and "The Psalm of the West" in his 1876 volume of poetry helped to establish Lanier as a cosmopolitan writer (neither poem made even the vaguest allusion to the South—apart from five fairly abstract stanzas in "The Psalm of the West"—though supposedly national and historical in scope) and freed him to write his new poetry, if he could.

IV   *"The Song of the Chattahoochee"*

Lanier's guidebook, *Florida* (1876), commissioned, ironically enough, by a railroad owner who had liked "Corn," served as a transition from his earlier attitudes toward nature. Naturally the *Nation* attacked it for its "rhetorical-poetical foible of seeing 'God in everything,'" as is shown in some similes. But Lanier had begun to express a new idea in this book; nature is an "everlasting Word" which reveals God is everything. In his wild river and in his mysterious marshes, Lanier adds to the beneficence, purposiveness, and harmony of nature a sublimity, while he continues the idea dramatized in *Tiger-Lilies* of nature as guide. His travel book had guided him toward a new handling of nature, one partly heralded by "Corn" and "The Symphony" but one incorporating the idea of the regeneration of nature and man that he had sporadically used for many years.

"The Song of the Chattahoochee" is a sharp departure from "Clover" and "The Waving of the Corn" of 1876. In the blank-verse "Clover" an ox, "Course of things," grazes on clover made of

the heads of Keats, Chopin, and others—a strained allegorical attack on boorish society that Lanier concludes serenely with the
assertion that "The artist's market is the heart of man." In "The
Waving of the Corn," the narrator desires to "Suck honey summer
with unjealous bees" in a pastoral retreat from the "terrible
Towns." Lanier's habitual opposition of God's nature and man's
town receives nearly no development and perhaps causes the eccentric imagery. But in "The Song of the Chattahoochee" the symbolic meaning arises through onomatopoetic representation of the
physical sublimity of the river. The movement of the river
through the romantic landscape to the sea is the moral imperative
of responsibility. But the moral is mainly implied, and the music
rather than the idea controls the poem. An improvement on the
sentimental piety of "seeing God in everything," Lanier found his
true voice again in this poem.

Since the poem was not in the first person in the first draft,
Lanier may have recognized that the poem would gain immedi-
acy if the river narrated its own trip. In his revision, he also chose
present over past tense, and he reinforced his action verbs and
long prepositional phrases to give the river a swooping speed:

1	Out of the hills of Habersham,
	Down the valleys of Hall,
	I hurry amain to reach the plain,
	Run the rapid and leap the fall,
5	Split at the rock and together again,
	Accept my bed, or narrow or wide,
	And flee from folly on every side
	With a lover's pain to attain the plain
	Far from the hills of Habersham,
10	Far from the valleys of Hall.[17]

In this stanza and throughout the poem, Lanier outdoes himself in
his ability to vary the meter, match and clash tone colors, create
structural effects, and link the movement of the river to his special
effects. Perhaps the first thing to notice is the exceptional ease or
"fluidity" with which the lines move through their four feet of
mainly anapestic substitution (line 8). Yet pulling against this is
the frequent trochaic substitution (lines 3, 4, 5, 9, and 10) and the
successive stresses of line 7, in which even "on" takes at least a

secondary stress. Facilitating this fluid movement are the use of duosyllables or polysyllables often broken by the foot stresses (of Hab/ersham), the lack of caesuras (line 6 is the exception), and the lack of hiatus (vowels or consonants the same in successive syllables: "a army"; "lone neck"). Alliteration (lines 4 and 5) and internal rhyme (line 8) also give propulsion to the lines. But it should be understood that these devices only assist the semantic meaning in the lines, for semantic meaning guides us to locate the prosodic elements which account for the speed with which we read. Because all his poetic devices help to give a kinesthetic sense of the river's movement, we could say that the river is physically represented through the onomatopoeia created by all those elements. For this reason the poem is a classic example of a perfect blending of sound and sense.

Some of the tone color is especially good. We notice how the staccato rhythm of "run the rapid" echoes the rapids themselves. A linkage between the phrases could easily have been made ("rapids"), but this would diminish the effect. The graceful but dissonant phrase "leap the fall" balances its alliterative cluster against "run the rapid." Additionally, *p* and *f* are consonantal cousins related to the *p* of "rapid." The two phrases are thus separated but subtly joined.

Lanier's rhymes show great ingenuity. The refrains that form opening and closing couplets of each stanza are naturally perfect rhymes. Lines 3 and 8 of each stanza are rhymed with the same words, and in these lines Lanier rhymes a medial word with the rhyme word in nine out of ten places in the poem. In line 8 of stanza four, there is no medial rhyme; but Lanier uses all vowels (*a-u-i-e-o*), substituting variety for the expected pattern. In the second stanza for additional variety he uses three consecutive rhyme words (two of which are the same) in lines 3 and 7—the same pattern used in line 7 of the first stanza. When Lanier discards one device, he usually emphasizes another: in stanza three, for example, at the turning of the poem, he uses internal rhyme in lines 3, 6, 7, 9, and 10 (the last one is an interlinear rhyme). But in stanza four there is no internal rhyme, while in the final stanza nearly every line has internal rhyme. A comparison with the rhyme of "The Symphony" shows how Lanier's penchant for rhyme had led him into a playfulness early in the strings section which underminded his serious thoughts. But in "The Song of the

Chattahoochee" the rhyme is exactly right; though the theme of
the poem is serious—the obedient response of nature to its higher
commands—the eagerness and excitement of the river as it fulfills
that theme are the real center of interest.

It has been observed that, although the anapestic meter gives
speed and urgency to the line (perhaps because we instinctively
read over unstressed syllables quickly in order to find the
stresses), Lanier had also employed frequent trochaic substitutions which tended to slow the line by placing the stress early in
the foot. Thus a resistance is created to the river's movement; and,
as we would expect, the resistance becomes actively embodied in
the imagery of the poem, as well as in other musical devices.

For in the second stanza as the idea of resistance enters the
poem, Lanier uses such a line as this to slow the line with caesura,
long vowels and hiatus: "And the little reeds sighed *Abide,
abide.*" In addition, every line in the stanza is end-stopped; it is
the only stanza without any enjambment. But in the third and
fifth stanzas, to increase the pace of the river's movement, Lanier
uses enjambment three times. To give some idea of the circuitous
route of the river in the third stanza, Lanier uses eight caesuras to
fragment the line; but the sense of the stanza is still a forward
movement because of the many other sound devices at work. The
refrain must not be overlooked as a source of that speed and fluidity; for, once we anticipate its position in the stanza, we gain a
sense of direction and "purpose." The first line of the refrain is
exactly one syllable longer than the second line in each of its ten
appearances, thereby giving a slightly top-heavy momentum to the
first line. Twice the eighth lines of the stanza run directly into
the refrain, in the first and fifth stanzas, and thus seemingly pours
the river into the sea. The prepositional phrases in the final stanza
beginning "Downward" carry greater weight than the lines in the
same position of previous stanzas. The trochees seem to suggest
not only determination but also that the journey of the river to its
Lord the sea is rapidly coming to its conclusion.

By such careful handling of poetic devices as these, Lanier
shows that his reputation for musical verse is so well deserved as
to assure him of continued attention.[18] And the success of this
poem ought not to be minimized, for Lanier found a way to educate feelings through the music of verse in many ways more effectively than he had in "The Symphony." For one thing, he was able

to insert detailed descriptions of nature, as he had in "The Symphony," but without letting the general direction of the poem become lax. He could imply the idea of the importance of feeling and of love through the river's obedient response to its Lord the sea without being excessively didactic. The poem easily admits the symbolic meaning of the soul's journey through a turbulent life toward peace or God. It is possible that the poem reflects Lanier's own growth of confidence and direction.

V Toward "The Marshes of Glynn"

After Lanier had gone North in 1873 to become a musician and poet, he spent almost all his time away from Macon. Not only was the South a poor place for artistic pursuits, but Georgia, ironically, had a dangerous climate for tuberculars. But, in 1875 and in 1877, he visited the marshes of Glynn County; his impressions, after incubating for three years, became the poem. In 1875, he wrote, "What more should a work-battered man desire, in this divine atmosphere which seems like a great sigh of pleasure from some immense Lotus in this vague South?" He contrasted the "clambering and twining things" to the "gloomy pines" of Pennsylvania, and he detected "secrets" in the leaves—images that entered directly into the first stanza of the poem. In 1877, he wrote to Bayard Taylor that every leaf bred a poem in him: "God help the world, when this now-hatching brood of my Ephemerae shall take flight and darken the air." [19] Oddly enough, none of his letters from Brunswick mention the marshes or the sea, the most troubling symbols of the poem and the ones which freed Lanier from his easy religious beliefs. Certainly, the meaning of the symbols came to him only during the process of creative composition. They forced him to recognize himself.

His experiences in Washington ("a place where only rascality can profit") and Baltimore, where he spent the summer of 1877 writing the poem, must have enforced his longing for Georgia and helped him find the essential qualities that had moved him so deeply but which, on being immersed in them, must have eluded him. At Chad's Ford, Pennsylvania, he found a "loveliness of wood, earth, and water" which made him feel he "could do the whole Universe into poetry," though he did not want to do anything "large" for a while. Within a year, he had written "The Marshes of Glynn," not his longest poem, but his greatest.

Lanier's sense of the spirituality of nature received significant
literary buttresses when he read Emerson and Whitman, apparently for the first time in 1877–78. In May, 1877, he wrote that
Emerson gave him "immeasurable delight" because he pro-
pounded no systems or creeds.[20] Emerson's essays, of course, had
always been an influence, but "A Florida Sunday" may show a
more direct response to Emerson than any of his other poetry;
and, coming shortly before the writing of the "Marsh" poems, it
shows the influence at work on Lanier.

"A Florida Sunday" links beauty, nature, and spirit in ways that
resemble Emerson's "Each and All." A vividly detailed picture of
nature leads to Transcendental synthesis:

> The grace of God made manifest in curves—
> All riches, goods and braveries never told
> Of earth, sun, air and heaven—now I hold
> Your being in my being; I am ye,
> And ye myself; yea, lastly, Thee,
> God, whom my roads all reach, howe'er they run.[21]

In his lectures on the English novel (1881), Lanier found in
Emerson's "Each and All" a subtle linking of truth and beauty;
but, interestingly enough, Emerson more successfully unites concrete and abstract; and, although Lanier quoted the following
lines in his lecture, he nevertheless pursued his own intuition in
his "Marsh" poems:

> Over me soared the eternal sky,
> Full of light and of deity;
> Again I saw, again I heard
> The rolling river, the morning bird;
> Beauty through my senses stole,
> I yielded myself to the perfect whole.[22]

By 1877, the Transcendentalism of Emerson's essays was more influential than that of his poetry, and Lanier had imbibed it, like
most American poets of the late nineteenth century, at second or
third hand. Emerson made the Transcendental imagination possible for a postwar world which was far less capable of taking it
seriously than his time had been.

Lanier was aware of Whitman by at least October 23, 1874,

when, according to Professor Anderson, he thought *The Galaxy* magazine wrong to hail Whitman as a genius. In January, 1875, Lanier wrote that the *Philadelphia Evening Bulletin,* in praising "Corn," had condemned "the trash and sensationalism of the 'dialect' poets, the Walt Whitmans and the Joaquin Millers." [23] At the end of the year he was shocked that Dante Gabriel Rossetti would swear that "Whitman is the greatest American Singer." Swinburne apparently also preferred Whitman. But, by February, 1878, Lanier came to agree when he finally read Whitman and wrote to Bayard Taylor that *Leaves of Grass* was "a real refreshment . . . like rude salt spray in your face." [24] Though he accuses Whitman of mistaking naturalness with goodness, and though he insists his own assumptions about art were worlds apart from Whitman's, he still sensed an original talent moving in roughly the same direction that he was—toward free verse—but for entirely different reasons.

In May, 1878, Lanier wrote to Whitman of his reactions, declaring that no other "modern song" struck him as "so large and so naive." He found it a lesson to "the time" of the integrity of the individual, and he commended Whitman's "beautiful rhythms." [25] But the public voice is not the private reflection, and in two outlines for poems Lanier sees Whitman as a symbol of "poetry's butcher," and in the same English-novel lecture in which he praised Emerson, he criticized Whitman for invading the realm of personality in literature because his art was "formless" and morally mistaken. Yet he found the poem that examined Lincoln's personalty, "O Captain, My Captain," to be "surely one of the most tender and beautiful poems in any language." Lanier's attraction to Whitman's one major "regular" poem suggests he responded to the subject—the death of a great man—without considering the style. Had Lanier thought more carefully about Whitman's poetry, he might have discovered in "When Lilacs Last in the Dooryard Bloom'd," a poem that closely resembled "The Marshes of Glynn" in its diffuse symbolism and in its musicality of verse—as well as a far better poem on the death of Lincoln.

Whitman's persona, the autobiographical character in his poems he resembles, must have struck Lanier as threatening because of its comprehensiveness and its simplicity. Whitman could use his "I" of "Song of Myself" in at least four separate ways—as

Walt the actual man, as a representative of humanity, as a natural man, and as the cosmic man of the future. Each of these is worlds apart from the anxious, doubting, pious, isolated persona Lanier uses in his "Marsh" poems. The supreme surety of Whitman's persona is just what Lanier's seeks. Whitman's man could speak for all men because he includes so much of life. But Lanier's most complex persona searches for his own soul; he does not stretch on the grass and invite his soul, confidently penetrating every aspect of humanity. Instead, Lanier's persona passes through existential anguish to religious serenity.

Lanier thus made the mistake of thinking that Whitman's openness to life was a radical flaw, complaining that he could find only that Whitman was "undemocratic," a "dandy," a slave of nature, and, he implies, a misguided fellow who thought sheer size to be everything. Worse than these, he thinks the body is the soul; and, though he insists he is religious, he reveals "no tenet, no rubric" except that man must be natural.[26] It is astounding that Lanier was unable to see Whitman's Transcendentalism. His criticism is such a distortion of Whitman's work that we can only think it severely threatened Lanier as a poet and a person, by suggesting that a totally different technique might in fact be the poetry of the future and by asserting what must have sounded like a poetry grounded in Locke, Adam Smith, Paley, Hamilton, and Kant—all those writers that Lanier had early seen as the most dangerous to art. We must deeply regret Lanier's inability, at this most serious juncture in his life, to see the greatness in Whitman and to learn from him. Lanier's artistic humility seems to have deserted him when he needed it most; but once again his rejection, like his rejections of Kant, Goethe, and Mozart, is instructive, for it shows how Lanier progressively narrowed his view of life so that he could squeeze from a few basic ideas enough faith to continue writing.

If he found Emerson's spiritual view of nature more compatible than Whitman's putative hedonism, Lanier nevertheless must have recognized that they were kindred spirits. The speaker of "The Marshes of Glynn," like the persona of "Song of Myself," takes Emerson's command to go into the woods to discover the self as his point of departure. Lanier followed his own command and went into a musically conceived nature to discover himself.

In 1878, at the Maryland Music Festival, six weeks before he wrote "The Marshes of Glynn," Lanier found that Beethoven's Symphony No. 7 summoned up images from nature. He found that the work showed the modern impulse of direct sympathy with nature, an idea earlier expressed in *Tiger-Lilies*, "Retrospects and Prospects," "The Symphony," and later in his Shakespeare lectures. Lanier's extensive description of Beethoven's symphony seems to use imagery of the sort he associated with Whitman: "the gigantic figure of jovial animality in Nature careering about the world of tone in unrestrained jubilation." This description of the fourth movement sees the energy of nature as essentially beneficent.[27]

His description of Wagner's "Siegfried Idyl" (he had written a poem to Wagner in 1877) prophetically suggested the form he would use in "The Marshes of Glynn": "First the violins give out a beautiful tune; presently from another side of the orchestra a different tune strikes in, then another from another side, and so on until every instrument is engaged simultaneously in playing independent tunes. To follow these through their sinuous windings and interweavings is possible only to a practised ear and concentrated attention." [28] In an analogous way, the poem would usher in various themes derived from different feelings of the persona so that their "sinuous windings and interweavings" take a practiced poetic ear to define.

VI *"The Marshes of Glynn"*

Lanier's greatest poem, "The Marshes of Glynn," combines all the musical complexity we have examined in "The Symphony" and in "The Song of the Chattahoochee" with a suddenly revitalized understanding of the spiritual regeneration he had used in the somewhat mythic "Corn." Taking a deeper plunge into subjective consciousness than ever before, he discovers the limits of freedom and self-knowledge in a persona who gives himself to feeling. Lanier's friendly critics have praised his music but have neglected his total achievement, while his hostile critics have accused him of symbolic obscurity and contrived versification. In the following analysis, I hope to present the claims of both sides and to offer a comprehensive defense of the poem which will help to illuminate the development of Lanier's creative process.

The first stanza immediately creates emotional relatedness between the persona and the reader through impressionistic details.

1   Glooms of the live-oaks, beautiful-braided and woven
      With intricate shades of the vines that myriad-cloven
          Clamber the forks of the multiform boughs,—
              Emerald twilights,—
                  Virginal shy lights,
      Wrought of the leaves to allure to the whisper of vows,
      When lovers pace timidly down through the green colonnades
          Of the dim sweet woods, of the dear dark woods,
              Of the heavenly woods and glades,
10   That run to the radiant marginal sand-beach within
          The wide sea-marshes of Glynn;—[29]

The variety of connections and disjunctions of vowels and consonants creates an ebb and flow, as the line lengths themselves, shaped by musical phrasings, onomatopoetically represent the form and shape of the rivulets. Although the persona has just entered the woods, his imagination already carries him forward to the marshes. The purpose of these many devices is to establish a state of feeling, and the extraordinarily long sentence length, carrying to line 36, creates a "suspension" of time, by its multi-subordination, its few independent constructions, and its few finite verbs. Although one critic has objected to this style because it obscures Lanier's argument, it is worth noting that the style *is* Lanier's argument; that is, his purpose is to establish the mystical power of the woods, not to present an ecological program or rules of woodcraft. The images of the stanza are organized like musical ideas in an impressionistic tone poem, blending perfectly to the free-form construction of the sentence. To capsulize, the form of the stanza (a microcosm of the intentions of the entire poem) aspires to the condition of music.

The opening of the poem is filled with associational images, some of which make sense, some of which are purely musical, but all of which are needed to sustain the feeling. "Virginal shy lights" is almost meaningless, semantically, but the music of the stanza would be weakened without it, since it creates a musical phrase which momentarily impedes the sweep of the dactyls. The phrase is not devoid of meaning, though objections can be raised to its coyness in, or to its pathetic fallacy of, likening the wood's light to a virgin's diffidence. "Emerald twilights" is suggestive but not concrete, though the stanza would lose some of its dreamlike radiance if the phrase were deleted. "When lovers pace timidly down though the green colonnades" is certainly precious, but it helps us visualize the diffuse sexual associations found throughout the stanza. Perhaps their stroll foreshadows the narrator's walk toward the marshes; if it does, then a metaphor distinguishing the peculiar texture of light in the woods has eventually provoked a journey toward the source of nature's mysteries, which, symbolically, is the Self. As Lanier said in his 1860 letter to his father, feeling precedes thought; and it also precedes religious conversion. Almost unconsciously, the narrator is beginning to form the thought of going deeper into the woods in order to arrive at the marshes and the sea and to discover the secret of nature and himself. He is off on the Transcendental adventure, lured by the beckoning phantom of nature.

Harry Warfel in "Mystic Vision in 'The Marshes of Glynn'" has argued that the structure of the poem is the mystic vision, somewhat mechanically listing the time scheme, tenses, narrative actions, and states of visions of the poem, as well as its syntax.[30] His article labels various sections of the poem according to their position on the chart of a mystic vision, from "Purgation in the forest temple" (lines 1–17) to "Union" and "Ecstasy" (lines 79–94 and 95–98). Though arrived at independently, Warfel's view and that proposed in this chapter have much in common; but he makes no inquiry into the psychological world of the narrator, and thus he says nothing about the sudden shift at the end of the poem when the narrator faces the puzzling "Forms that swim and shapes that creep" in the marsh rivulets. I intend to show that the persona's psychological world is the crux of Lanier's view of the morality of feeling. And it is also a rationale for the musicality of the poem.

More significantly, although Warfel calls the poem "program poetry," on the model of "program music," he does not attend to the music of the poem, though he insists Lanier integrated "all the elements of image and music" available to a poet. To a great extent, this musicality creates the Transcendental character of the narrator; but only a careful, even elaborate, analysis can fully reveal Lanier's unusual music. The first stanza embodies all of the complexities of the music, so our study of it may serve as representative of the poem's music.

The music of the poem affects us at once. Naturally, alliteration and assonance of all sorts are everywhere apparent in this seemingly endless sentence, which goes on for twenty-five more lines.

But more subtle is the echoic alliteration in lines 1, 2, and 3 where "glooms," "cloven," and "clamber" are linked; and they attach themselves finally to "Glynn," the last word of this section. The cluster reappears with variation in phrases like "green colonnades." And the rhythm of the first musical phrase is picked up in the fourth and fifth lines, and a rather clever connection is made between them by the feminine double rhyme which characterizes lines 1, 2, 4, and 5. We might note also that "emerald" and "virginal" have a very subtle linking together through the family of M and N consonants. Another rather nice touch is the use of weak-ending rhyme that always precedes the line ending, "marshes of Glynn."

As in "The Song of the Chattahoochee," the number of syllables of similarly indented lines is usually overbalanced, the first line containing one syllable more than the next. Since such lines are usually separated by others of longer or shorter length, Lanier keeps the over-balancing graceful. (See lines 3 and 8, 9 and 11.) The occurrence of feminine rhyme in this stanza helps to produce a meditative tone. Feminine endings also supply a softness of feeling, blending rather nicely to the first and tenth lines which use resonant consonants (m, z, n) with the liquids (l, r, w). The phrase "marshes of Glynn" is exceptionally resonant. Meanwhile, Lanier often employs sounds of "breathiness" (h, f, v, th, s, ch, sh), as in the ninth line, to give a sense of wonder or astonishment. The long vowels throughout the stanza lend quiet dignity.

Until now the woods had symbolized the accustomed healing power of nature and the Emersonian "emblem" through which God appears. Now the narrator recalls a day in the past when he had experienced a moment of ecstasy at the forces of nature. The suggestion hovers that the narrator is thus attempting to re-create a previous experience, supporting the argument that the speed of the rhythms look forward to the marshes, while the sounds of the words cast the spell of the woods. Again, does the "noon-day" sun signify youth and innocence, contrasted to the "slant yellow beam" of age and experience? Lanier's diffuse imagery suggests a good deal; but, because of the nature of the state of feeling he chose to delineate, he does not offer explicit resolution of these possibilities.

Apparently, the narrator had withdrawn during the "noon-day" into the balm of nature, for he had been too fearful to approach the marshes. But now he is, for unstated reasons, prepared. We discover at the end of the poem that his fear of the marshes was well warranted; for, as Ross has suggested, "The very openness and spaciousness of the marsh, indeed, make it a particularly apt symbol for much that poets found disturbing in nineteenth century science." [31] But Lanier is not Thomas Hardy, and the marshes of Glynn are not Egdon Heath. The protean quality of nature may create a sensuous delight, but it can leave one with a sense of the ultimate unknowableness of nature. Such are the marshes and the heath (and Moby Dick). But, as we shall see, like Philip Sterling of *Tiger-Lilies,* Lanier's persona decides to love nature though he cannot understand it.

These musical devices of phonetic-iteration tend to slow down the lines, giving them weight and even majesty. Adding to this effect is the use of several strong stresses, suggesting deep thoughts, in single lines; lines 1 and 2 have six beats; and line 20 ("Ye held me fast in your heart and I held you fast in mine") contains at least eight. The use of successive stresses, as in line 20, lends emphasis to several syllables and thus retards the line. But, oddly enough, the meter of the poem seems to counter these effects of stateliness and meditation. The strong dactylic lines create much the same quick movement as the anapestic lines of "The Song of the Chattahoochee."

Like "The Song," "The Marshes" also uses alliteration and internal rhyme and few caesuras. But it does not use many monosyllables (line 20 is a notable exception) or employ hiatus or phrases that are hard to articulate. All these things give the lines an ease of movement. But, of most importance, Lanier does not use the ideas of movement or of rest in the poem; and so, from the beginning, there seem to be opposed responses created in the reader—a sense of speed and urgency, created through the meter and the stresses primarily, is placed in apparent opposition to the somber, reflective tone arising from the deliberate use of phonetic-iteration.

Yet the apparent contradiction can be resolved. The narrator's impulse is toward the marshes; and hence his thoughts seem to be shaped according to his emotional re-creation of them. These thoughts reflect the very form and shape of the marshes' rivulets, and they also suggest the movement of the water when the tide

comes in (as it does at the end of the poem). But the woods
through which the persona passes strike him also and inspire reverie, awe and, as we shortly learn, fear. His immediate state of
mind and his anticipated state of mind are brought together.

As the narrator continues his reverie in the second stanza, the
woods take on a more specific religious imagery than previously:
they become a monastery with "closets of lone desire" and "Cells
for the passionate pleasure of prayer to the soul that grieves, /
Pure with a sense of the passing of saints through the woods." The
woods are thus sensuous and spiritual, as his letter of 1875 dis-
closed—the bifurcated vision of all Transcendental poets. The
mundane lover is now the lover of God; and the narrator in
the third stanza praises the woods once again, recapitulating the
opening lines, but with this difference:

> . . . now, when my soul all day hath drunken the soul of the oak,
>   And my heart is at ease from men, and the wearisome sound
>   of the stroke
>   Of the scythe of time and the trowel of trade is low,
>   And belief overmasters doubt, and I know that I know,
>   And my spirit is grown to a lordly great compass within,
> 30 That the length and the breadth and the sweep of the
>   marshes of Glynn
>   Will work me no fear like the fear they have wrought me
>   of yore

Unafraid, he steps from his cover with chivalric fealty.

> 42   Affable live-oak, leaning low,—
>   Thus—with your favor—soft, with a reverent hand,
>   (Not lightly touching your person, Lord of the land!)

He moves to the domain of another Lord, and is once again capti-
vated by the physical beauty of the place:

>   Sinuous southward and sinuous northward the shimmering
>   band
> 50 Of the sand-beach fastens the fringe of the marsh to the folds
>   of the land.
>   Inward and outward to northward and southward the beach-
>   lines linger and curl

As a silver-wrought garment that clings to and follows the firm
    sweet limbs of a girl.
Vanishing, swerving, evermore curving again into sight,
Softly the sand-beach wavers away to a dim gray looping of
    light.

Again, the coy image of the girl's garment (prepared for by
"fringe" and by the lovers in the woods) nearly undoes some powerful descriptive details. But, just as the lovers led him to the
marsh, so does the motion of the girl's limbs draw his eye down
the beach to the magnificent spaciousness of the marshes. She
seems to be a clumsy transformation of the "Brown Dusk," nature's spirit of *Tiger-Lilies*. It should be clear that, though Lanier's
images are often sentimental or even grotesque, he finds ways to
make them work. Here they help to concretize the abstract view
of the marshes.

An interesting complication arises as this long third stanza
closes:

55 And what if behind me to westward the wall of the woods
        stands high?
    The world lies east: how ample, the marsh and the sea and
        the sky!

Oddly, the woods now seem to pose a threat which is, of course,
disclaimed at once. Why? Because the woods represent the refuge, perhaps Eden, and the innocence which cannot be recovered,
though it may still be attractive. But purity is more than innocence, and the marshes promise purity. Thus, Ross is mistaken in
thinking that Lanier has used the woods in contradictory ways:
first, as a symbol of spiritual enlightenment; second, as a symbol
of fear. The persona's perspective has radically altered, and hence
a natural shift in his evaluation of the woods follows. Ross has
asked that Lanier's symbols be "crystal clear and consistent," but
this request would limit the rich suggestiveness Lanier wants to
create through the diffusion of his effects. Anyway, as the narrator
has shown, the woods never entirely healed his fears; apparently,
he recovered his strength in the world where "the weighing of fate
and the sad discussion of sin" is possible. Ross assumes what
Lanier does not show—that these woods are the beneficent healing woods of Bryant, Wordsworth, or Emerson.

In the fourth stanza, the metaphorical descriptions of the marshes are presented in paradoxes:

67   Tolerant plains, that suffer the sea and the rains and the sun,
      Ye spread and span like the catholic man who hath mightily
          won
          God out of knowledge and good out of infinite pain
          And sight out of blindness and purity out of a stain.

Robert Penn Warren thinks these lines almost meaningless, but they are the traditional paradoxes of religious conversion placed in terms of a comparison between the human soul and natural imagery, qualified by adjectives that invite the pathetic fallacy by facile personification. Lanier defines here the equality of spirit possessed by the "great man" he had long prophesied would liberate his mistaken age.

The religious imagery has moved from the woods as a monk's cell to the more liberating marshes (the forty-seventh line contains one word in describing the narrator's feeling on stepping on the sand: "Free"). And now the marsh-hen indirectly provides a glimpse of God Himself, while it also symbolizes the narrator's soul on a heavenward flight:

71   I will fly in the greatness of God as the marsh-hen flies
      In the freedom that fills all the space 'twixt the marsh and
          the skies:
75   By so many roots as the marsh-grass sends in the sod
      I will heartily lay me a-hold on the greatness of God:
      Oh, like to the greatness of God is the greatness within
      The range of the marshes, the liberal marshes of Glynn.

Ross has suggested that the passage is weakened by the shift from metaphor to simile: since the narrator claims he will fly in the greatness of God, then it is presumably misleading to say the marshes are only "like to the greatness of God." Lanier is obviously thinking of the regenerative possibilties of God's greatness. In fact, the marsh-hen is simply a concrete "emblem" stimulating meditation on God's greatness. Identification with God by way of nature has superseded the impressionistic intimations of Him in the first stanza. Lanier's exuberance, however, has temporarily presumed too much, and by the poem's end he will redefine the limits of his knowledge and freedom.

At this point, Ross's structural criticism should be noted. He senses an imbalance between stanzas dealing with the woods, the marsh, and the sea; but he does not say why balance between the sections is desirable in *this* poem. If we were to formalize the three as symbols of, say, body, mind, and spirit, then perhaps a symmetrical balance would satisfy our conventional expectations. But Lanier deals with the symbols according to their psychological relevance for disclosing the deepest states of moral feeling— not according to a routine method of organization.

The sea is used least of the three major symbols, but it is the mysterious source of the marsh's "uttermost creeks" and mediator between the marsh and the source of life, the sun:

80   Look how the grace of the sea doth go
       About and about through the intricate channels that flow
           Here and there,
           Everywhere,
   Till his waters have flooded the uttermost creeks and the low-
       lying lanes,
       And the marsh is meshed with a million veins,
    That like as with rosy and silvery essences flow
       In the rose-and-silver evening glow.
         Farewell, my lord Sun!

The setting sun produces the rising tide, and the chivalric farewell reminds us that the narrator has adopted the necessary humility with which to confer with nature. A "hurrying sound of wings that westward whirr" sends the marsh-hen to heaven as a symbol of the narrator's soul. The dramatic situation is the same as the end of "The Symphony," but the symbolic bird does not sail over a "waste." It is no longer necessary to assert the relationship between music and love since the entire poem has used music to illuminate the search for self-love and divine love. Night falls.

The cycle of day has run its course, and the spiritual life of man has been traced from its early fears to a growing trust and a symbolic ascent. And yet at the final moment, Lanier's optimism falters. This faltering sends an inspired poem toward greatness. For, in the sudden doubts on the threshold of eternity, Lanier reunites himself to the desperate, pious, and sensitive men who counter the materialism of their time to try to discover themselves but who lack the extraordinary confidence of the "great men." Such men—divorced from the communal values which customarily promote a sense of identity and give purpose to life—seem quite unlikely candidates for becoming the men who lead their society from its error of undervaluing feelings. Though Lanier would publicly say otherwise, the end of this poem shows that he had probably given up his imitation of Christ in order to take part in the tragic sense of life. The protean symbols of the last stanza show that man can have no absolute knowledge; therefore, he can concoct no symbols of absolute truths.

99   And now from the Vast of the Lord will the waters of sleep
                Roll in on the souls of men,
            But who will reveal to our waking ken
            The forms that swim and the shapes that creep
                Under the waters of sleep?
    And I would I could know what swimmeth below when the
                tide comes in
        On the length and the breadth of the marvellous marshes
                of Glynn.

We notice how the first two lines (99 and 100) move quickly with their regular anapests and iambs in a rising rhythm. But the question (line 101) nearly freezes because of the many strong stresses. The archaic word "ken" seems to resonate throughout the next monosyllabic line to produce a profound sense of understated meditation. Rounding off this effect is the next line, which begins with an arresting dactyl and repeats "under the waters of sleep" for emphasis. Those who accuse Lanier of sentimentality would do well to observe how he underplays the anxiety in this stanza.

But Ross, like others, has sensed the apparent failure of so dark a conclusion for a Transcendental nature poem: "How can the poet's comparison of the tide to the 'waters of sleep' be considered relevant to this particular poem in this particular context?" He feels the poem would end better with the falling of night and with the completion of the existential experience of the poem. The final seven lines seem to Ross to be "a logical and aesthetic non sequitur." He suggests that possibly "the forms that swim and the shapes that creep" may be precursors of Freudian symbols liberated by the unconscious mind. Perhaps he is right; but it is also another way to express the relation of the man of feeling to the man of spiritual feeling. Yet it seems unlikely that Lanier saw the destructive forces of irrationality below the spiritual veil of the sea. He saw, the evidence suggests, much more: the destructive forces in nature itself, which may account for the errors of his age. Lanier would never have accepted the implied determinism of irrational forces in man, but he could admit that there may be forces in nature which are beyond man's grasp which make it impossible for him to realize his finest ideals of selfhood. Lanier's dark night of the soul is neither a logical nor an esthetic non sequitur.

Ross has also offered an historical explanation for Lanier's inability to condemn or condone the marshes as spiritual guides: the fear of cosmic space and of evolutionary history which left nineteenth-century man doubtful about the efficacy of "seeing God in everything." Ross finds this conflict in Melville and in some major poets, and it is of course a hallmark of Naturalism. Though he did project the basic tension of his age, the conflict between empiricism and Transcendentalism, Lanier did not see the problem in Ross's terms.

Instead, "The Marshes of Glynn" explores the human limitations which define man's spiritual quest. So long as Lanier's persona blindly accepted the goodness of woods, marsh, and sea, he felt no anguish. Yet there were intimations of some nameless fear or dread of the marshes in previous trips to the woods. But Lanier clearly thought that only the truth could set men free and that true education of feeling might lay in being capable of accepting the most sobering truths.

Lanier's earlier uses of the "forms that swim" metaphor may help to establish some perspective. His four previous employments reveal a growing awareness. In *Tiger-Lilies*, Felix Sterling's soul conceals "in its immense translucency myriads of unknown things." But music causes "all the sea-shapes, terrible and beautiful together" to rise "in strange shoals to the surface." [32] Music thus draws strange forms from even a stereotypical saint like Felix, and this effect foreshadows her father John Sterling's telling Ottilie that "the heart will find behind Nature love as well as terror, and will spring to the most powerful of these, which is love." [33] Had Lanier meant to explore this idea closely, he might have shown what John Sterling thought of the war which unmercifully destroyed him and his wife and home. Lanier is speaking of a love that conquers all.

But in 1872 he was not so sure that the dark forces in nature could be so easily dispelled. Writing to Virginia Hankins (to whom he had once proposed), he refuted her notion that life glides away like a river: "but . . . the hopes, the fears . . . the strange shelled creatures, the marvelous freaks and glories that exist in the depth of the sea-water;—do *these* glide away?" [34] But Lanier does not answer his curious rhetorical question, the essence of which seems to be that strange emotions in man's nature cannot be neglected or ignored. Man must accept the totality of his nature.

Finally, the "Maryland Music Festival" essay synthesizes these ideas. Lanier compares the themes of Wagner's "Siegfried Idyll" to fish swimming in a pool:

> . . . a subdued flash here and there below the surface of the water calls our attention to dimly outlined forms swimming underneath; then the whole brilliant shoal rises to the top and shines in the sunlight, as in those glorious *crescendos* . . . then the shoal again sinks, the dark forms of the fish move hither and thither under the water, and finally all disappear. [35]

The dark forms of the fish mystify only because they are not sunlit. Day will prove it is right to believe in the goodness of feeling, but here on this dark earth we can only model our feelings on the symbols of moral guidance that most comprehensively disclose man's nature. Alone beneath a spacious dark sky and stranded by mysterious waters, the narrator of "The Marshes of Glynn" can be grateful for his extraordinary capacities of feeling which can allow him to probe deeply into his puzzling interior world.

And yet the images of the essay chart positive feelings because the music had reached toward a "glorious crescendo." But life is not art; and, though the narrator of the poem apparently puts his faith in nature despite his worries, the artistic form he would need to shape his understanding is indeed a "form that swims." Lanier continued to explore these marshes in his last poems for some possible clue to the final education of feelings that would restore the certainty of his youth. Lacking a sense of Southern community, unable to accept the sectionalism of the North though he had written its laudatory centennial verse, and unable to go deeper into his absorption with subjective states of feeling to assert a pure musicality and a diffuse imagery which became more private in its symbolism—Lanier was at an impasse. In his last two years, he had little to look forward to other than an embroidering of the relations of art, nature, and morality which he had early stumbled upon and later developed with a unique voice that made him one of the nineteenth century's major poets.

Within two years, Lanier had developed enormously. No longer capable of being contented with the facile optimism of the commissioned poetry of 1876 or with the minor if masterful effects of "The Song of the Chattahoochee," Lanier had learned to provoke the feelings of his audience subtly and powerfully, while exploring the possibilities of the mythic journey from land to sea, from personality to soul. It was not really necessary to develop the older theme of the regeneration of the land, for the poet's regeneration of spirit embodied a relation to nature that assumed nature's wholeness. Lanier had embarked on a program of self-education long before, but "The Marshes of Glynn" was real evidence that he had at last recognized that to achieve his education of feelings he would need to risk more than his craft—he would have to risk himself. A short poem outline, perhaps the last thing he ever wrote, can suggest the significance of the poem to him: "For I deemed it was safer not to depart from hence before I had acquitted my conscience with the composition of some poems in obedience to the dream." [36] The result of such dedication, "The Marshes of Glynn," was a poem with integrity of vision.

CHAPTER 7

Sunrise and Sunset:
"Obedience to the Dream"

IN his last years Lanier matched the tuberculosis that scorched
his lungs to a white-hot pen. Though he wrote in a continuous
streak, he was often forced by necessity to depart from projects
which might have continued the philosophical, psychological, and
esthetic investigations of "The Marshes of Glynn." In his last three
years only a few poems and *The Science of English Verse* continued the lines of his major development. But everything he
wrote still related itself directly to his dream of educating the
emotions of his nation and of correcting the mistaken devaluation
of feeling.

Lanier published "The Marshes of Glynn" in an omnibus volume of anonymous writers, *A Masque of Poets*. The book slipped
into oblivion because of the mediocrity of most of the selections,
but at least one reader thought Lanier's poem was by Tennyson.
And W. D. Howells, ironically enough, stated that it almost bet-
tered Swinburne.[1] Interestingly, though Lanier had read Swinburne and had frequently commented about him, he complained
that he could never be recognized in "a Swinburnian time." Though
he may have responded to Swinburne's rhythms and tone color, he
must have been displeased by the English poet's voluptuousness
and simple glitter.[2] Lanier had made his private amalgam of
Poe, Keats, Tennyson, Swinburne, Emerson, and Whitman; and
his poem was selected by Longfellow for his *Poems of Places*
(1879), perhaps because it appealed to his own rich sense of
rhythmic experimentation. For the past century, Lanier's fame has
rested on his musicality of verse, but it is unfortunate that no
commentator has recovered the thematic service Lanier's musical-

ity had performed. It had provoked a deeper emotional response for his fairly elementary ideas about the morality of feeling.

I   The Science of English Verse

During 1878 Lanier organized his many ideas on the interaction of music and poetry into a series of lectures at the Peabody Institute later published as *The Science of English Verse*. Even while at Oglethorpe, Lanier had been interested in the impact of music on feeling, and his musical career showed a determination to synthesize the two arts in accordance with what he felt to be the spirit of the time, as well as his personal religious aspirations.

Though virtually all poets have manipulated the musicality of verse, Lanier always placed a high priority on sonic rather than semantic effects of language. His debates, speeches, letters, and essays show conscious manipulation of dialects, speech rhythms, and phrasings of words. But he was determined to connect music and poetry, though, as seen in the previous chapter, when he had the chance to write poetry for music he failed. He thought his ideas in *The Science of English Verse* were original contributions to understanding verse technique, and he was right, though his work was misconstrued because of the book's ambiguous writing. It must have occurred to him that the demonstration of identities between music and poetry could subtly propagandize for the mysterious effect of music on the moral nature of man.

In selecting the term "science," Lanier was also ambiguous, though perhaps not intentionally misleading; for critics at once condemned him for trying to formulate with finality the ways poetry is constructed. He really only wanted to demonstrate some of the practices that have been followed and to suggest others. It has been thought that Lanier probably did not mean "verse" but "versification," for he does not deal with a large number of elements of verse which have little to do with versification. To Lanier, verse is simply the relation of sounds, so all that distinguishes music from poetry is the tone color of vowels and consonants compared to the tone color of flutes or violins. Both music and speech share rhythm, tune, and tone color; and, for this reason, poetry can gain some of the freedom of music.

As music may shift accent for emphasis away from the rhythmic accent, poetry can create an opposition between rhythmic and logical accent by use of originality in the creation of rhythms. (Lanier means that the stresses in a word may counter the rhythm of a line by having the divisions of a word of two or more syllables form separate parts of different musical groups, like the foot.) The freest poetry would have the least rhythmic regularity, the fewest end-stops in a line, and few strong line endings. In his implication that the freest poetry would tend toward prose—or what we now know as "free verse"—Lanier was creating the esthetic basis for much later experimentation; and he was also defining the nature of practices like Whitman's. Yet Lanier argued that such freedom would not create "prose poetry" since the freest poetry would be led back to poetry by the regularity of its rhythm. Interestingly, these arguments had occurred to Lanier not from an analysis of his or his contemporaries' techniques but from his study of Shakespeare's poetic development toward freer forms.

But Lanier did considerably more than merely insist upon the relation of music and poetry. For one thing, he presented the first lucid description of the way in which poetry could be understood according to musical rhythms, offering conclusive examples and detailed analysis. The poet Karl Shapiro has defended the work as "the most famous and influential in the field of temporal prosody . . . in no sense dated . . . one of the best expositions of its theory in the literature of metrics." [3] Most critics agree. Lanier was the first American to break ground for a richer understanding of poetic rhythm, and he is still important, as Joseph Hendren has shown in his recent thoughtful study, "Time and Stress in English Verse with Special Reference to Lanier's Theory of Rhythm." [4]

Hendren has found that Lanier's only fault is his inability to do away with the devices of traditional scansion and, therefore, rely completely on the musical implications of his novel approach. For Lanier intended to demonstrate how rhythm in poetry depends on the temporal relation of accents, and thus a different stress notation had to be used to make this apparent, a stress system using musical notation. This notation involves him in a demonstration of the difference in the "quantity" of syllables. Thus "it is" is an iambic unit like "was grouped," but the second "iamb" obviously takes longer to say than the first. There is a quantitative difference; and, since this is true, it is misleading to say they have the same foot length. Lanier assumed it would be possible for the trained ear to grasp spontaneously the similarities and differences of duration, but laboratory studies by linguists have shown, though there may be general agreement about many specific cases, the identifications of duration are subjective and variable. Even so, musical notation will give, in some ways, a clearer indication of exactly what rhythm is being employed than the stress-accent system does.

And so Lanier lists several rhythms of English verse according to how the ear instinctively groups sounds. Primary rhythm is the ticking of a clock before any pattern is imposed on it (tick-tick). Secondary rhythm is a pattern of clock ticks (tick-tock). Then Lanier sets up a system of proportions. If the second sound or syllable is twice, three times, or four times the previous one, then duple, triple, or quadruple time is constructed—exactly as in music. Lanier notes that a major difference between the musical and prosodic bar is that the musical one always begins with a stress or beat; yet it would have been easy for him to free himself from the necessity to adhere to the old system of the metrical foot and to scan his poetry fully in musical terms, as Hendren has suggested.

Lanier's other kinds of rhythm are not very useful, and, regretfully, he did not explore alliteration or assonance beyond a few preliminary notes. Yet his demonstration of the ability to scan poetry differently gave a sharp incentive to other investigations and made the musical study of verse a permanent part of English prosody.

Paul Fussell, Jr., has directed attention to basic problems involved in Lanier's approach when he notes the basic weakness in the added complexity of musical notation, as well as the danger of implying that poetry follows musical principles explicitly.[5] Allen Tate had earlier sounded the alarm by suggesting that a poet who would develop such a theory simply rationalizes his incapacity to take the subject matter of poetry seriously.[6] (In Tate's later essays, he seems unsure that poetry has a definable "subject matter.") Robert Penn Warren has accused Lanier of a complex camouflaging of his own withdrawal into feeling. Other critics have specifically attacked Lanier's inability to show in musical notation what is actually heard. But many scholars and poets have found that Lanier's theory redeems poetry from mechanical contrivances like the foot that are inaccurate and ambiguous; and we may cite the controversy among Lanier critics about the "meter" of "The Song of the Chattahoochee" and "The Marshes of Glynn." They have also found that Lanier's theory helps represent more accurately the different musical effects of the same kinds of feet.

Hendren's purpose was to "rescue Lanier's significant work from discredit and neglect," and he succeeds quite well. He begins by listing some basic errors, three of which are "that one can discover the rhythm of a verse by simply dividing it into feet," and "that a foot is a definable entity, or that accent (stress) in itself sufficiently accounts for rhythm." He emphasizes the importance of Lanier's description of the duration of sounds by showing that two dactylic lines may take different times to speak, one in duple time and another in triple. Thus, the same feet might have the difference of a waltz and a march, but conventional scansion would never indicate it. Additionally, the traditional foot is often helpless in dividing some lines—as many in "The Marshes of Glynn" might indicate. The foot itself, he concludes, "is not a section beginning with a stress, nor a section ending with a stress, nor an isochronous interval, nor a sense section, nor a syntactic grouping. Just what it is nobody can tell." [7] Lanier had begun to liberate prosody from fetters like the foot, but he had insisted on trying to construct a musical theory within the traditional use of the barred foot, a convention which his theory totally opposed.

Hendren reconstructs the direction of Lanier's thought and qualifies his overstatements. Lanier had said, "There is absolutely no difference between the sound-relations used in music and those used in verse," and he was quickly dismissed by many critics for his absolutism. He meant only "sound-relations," not actual performances or readings which, of course, draw in the element of subjectivity, according to Hendren. He also discusses Lanier's crucial core idea that "rhythm of any sort is impossible except through the coordination of time," and he explains that this means that "rhythm is neither performable nor conceivable without measured time; that every line of verse is divided into a number of sensibly equal time periods marked by stress; that the time periods so marked are themselves subdivided into equal segments of time (beats) by their syllable configuration." Here is the foundation of verse rhythm, and not only is Lanier right about it, but Hendren sees "the consensus of modern prosody" solidly behind him.

Lanier's major weaknesses in his theory now appear to be attributable to exaggeration. His title proclaimed what he knew could never be—a "science" of verse. His frequent and hasty comments about the place of quantity in English scansion that opposed his own practice surely show his manifesto fervor outrunning his good sense. Lanier did not want to describe merely the operations of music in poetry but how poetry began to etherealize by becoming like music. While his "wider applications" and perorations scattered through the book may have been simply oratorical embellishments, Lanier clearly wished to give music a more glorious place in man's life than others had. The examples he offered of the operation of music in ordinary life appealed to moral thinkers, and this effect was the major intention in Lanier's writing of this book: he intended to discover the ways in which emotion might be more completely manipulated. In a sense, the ultimate meaning of *The Science of English Verse* in the development of Lanier's imagination is similar to that of "The Marshes of Glynn."

One of Lanier's perorations shows this more clearly than this technical analysis of the book has perhaps done. He argues that science has proved that the primordial mode of disease, of the seasons, and of the distribution of nebulae—all things in "nature" —is rhythm. He points to Poe's view of the universe in *Eureka* as "nothing more than the rhythmic beating of the heart of God," and he calls it one of the most striking similes in literature. Paraphrasing his earlier comment in *Tiger-Lilies* that music is harmony, harmony is love, and love is God, Lanier quotes: " 'The father of metre is rhythm, and the father of rhythm is God.' " [8] As the action of opposing forces in nature and poetry creates rhythm, so natural oppositions in the moral world create "moral rhythm." Lanier put these thoughts into a poem, "Opposition," and this suggests that his perorations for his quite technical book were "prose poems." And yet Lanier, when revising his ideas for poems, chose, surprisingly, to follow the form of Tennyson's "In Memoriam" quatrains—iambic tetrameter rhyming *abab*.

As Lanier gained increased confidence from his experiments in "Corn" and "The Symphony," experiments which he thought placed him in the avant-garde, he felt that his poetry was beginning to shuck the bonds of convention. He perhaps made the mistake of many other poets in thinking that whatever is new is better and that "forms" necessarily suppress an ambitious poet's talents. Nevertheless, he succeeded in liberating himself from the mechanical schemes of meter and tone color that he had used in his poetry of the chivalric vein. He knew why he was liberating himself, so there was no danger of affectation or of the creation of "art-for-art's-sake" "esthetic poetry" which he despised. But Lanier's powerful hold on his view of the morality of feelings kept him from liberating his lexicon. He retained not only the archaisms with their implications of chivalric values but also some sentimental diction ("dear," "sweet") while he continued to manipulate imagery of nature.

It seems possible that Lanier's experiments with musical verse and his writing of The Science of English Verse were his ways of convincing himself that he was an original poet. For this reason his lexicon remained, apparently, more conventional even though his rhythms were so free that they moved toward free verse. He did not realize that such a verse called for a refinement in diction, tone, and imagery. Nor did he guess that his occasional grotesque images would become valuable to another kind of poet. In other words, Lanier was not a Symbolist poet; he simply moved along parallel lines with others who were in many ways precursors of it, like Swinburne, a translator of Baudelaire. Perhaps now the deeper tension in Lanier's mind has been exposed—reactionary imagery and diction opposed to a radical symbolism and musicality of verse. Growing more subjective, he intended to plan entire books of poetry around his "Marsh" poems. He had simply reached the limit of his vision and ability.

II Shakespeare

Lanier addressed The Science of English Verse to his fellow poets, and it surely appealed to them far more than his lectures on Shakespeare, those on the English novel, or his editions of chivalric classics—all works that resulted from Lanier's growing academic pursuits. While some may imagine these publications were unfortunate scatterings of his draining energy and dwindling time, Lanier seems to have taken this direction to confirm his basic ethical and esthetic ideas and to acquire a perspective from which to examine his literary situation. We may speculate that Lanier might have become increasingly absorbed by his nonpoetical interests and gradually stopped writing poetry completely. Perhaps he theorized that the lectern offered a better place from which to influence directly the morality of his age. Possibly Lanier might have been led to stop writing poetry if he had understood the depth of resistance in society to his evangel of love, and if he had recognized how his absorption in the musicality of verse had brought him close to the "art-for-art's-sake" decadence he despised.

His first serious interest in literary criticism took him naturally enough to Shakespeare; and, reflecting the "Bardolatry" of his time, Lanier thought Shakespeare the perfect synthesis of artistic originality and moral growth. Always a person who identified with great artists, Lanier may have found his "ego ideal" in Shakespeare. No matter what the reason, he found in Shakespeare's plays "moral teaching . . . pure morality" and that each play was "in the strictest sense, a powerful sermon." [9] Thus, *Two Gentlemen from Verona* (an unlikely choice) was to Lanier a "sermon" about "that forgiveness which pardons the trespasser." He found the greatest moral artist was also "a special adorer of music," so his life was "morally musical." Shakespeare's career moved from realism toward the "sweet music" of his last plays which centered on the theme of reconciliation and forgiveness. This theme, coincidentally, was also the major one of Lanier's last poems.

But Shakespeare's own moral growth, not his plays, interested Lanier, especially in its revelation through his changing poetic practices. Shakespeare's disuse of rhyme and regular rhythm and his use of run-on lines, feminine endings, and weak endings were "clearly an advance towards *freedom*." While Lanier's critical evaluation is correct, he makes a too-simple analogy from this fact when he asserts that Shakespeare's freedom enabled him to shift from "form toward chaos" and from love to egoism. But he finds that the great accomplishment of Shakespeare is his balancing of form against chaos in both art and morality, through a career that developed from the innocent relation of man to nature (*A Midsummer Night's Dream*), to the dark reality of man's relation to man (*Hamlet*), to the heavenly relation of man to God (*The Tempest*).[10] The pattern shows, not surprisingly, a great similarity to that of Lanier's own life work.

Lanier makes a tighter identification with Shakespeare by seeing him as opposed by the same vicious critics he had earlier delineated as kin to Christ's crucifiers. Lanier imagines that each of them was a prophet of a new poetry who was ignored by his age but who will be vindicated by the judgment of time. Lanier regards Shakespeare as having passed through the strains of oppositions on the way to forgiveness as Christ had. A diagram of the final plays resembled, to Lanier, a cross. Shakespeare was God's representative on earth, entrusted with teaching men how to control, "with temperance and perfect art," all oppositions.[11] Before the poet can teach, he must learn; but Lanier evidently did not see the relevance of his own writing of poetry to self-education, though he assumes that Shakespeare's life-work revealed such a self-education. Having made so many correspondences between himself and Shakespeare, it is likely that he would have seen that Shakespeare's loosening of forms resembled his own attempt to unite poetry to music.

III   *Forgiveness, the Last Major Theme*

As we have noted, Lanier asserted that Shakespeare's last phase used freer forms, and it centered upon the theme of forgiveness. The two were related in Lanier's mind. When the artist had achieved his "musical morality" through a struggle with artistic form which was, in fact, a moral struggle, he would then be able to confer this moral freedom on those who had never understood him, morally or artistically. In forgiving his detractors, he would relieve them of the guilt of having injured him, and he would also free himself from spite and anger. Put in other terms, the freedom to discover the limits of artistic possibilities required a strong capacity of self-identification. And this message, perhaps, was Lanier's final one about the education of the feelings of his age: by witnessing the artist's capacity for love and forgiveness, despite society's resistance, the men of the mistaken age could use him as a moral exemplar. Symbolic moral teaching is all that is left, and the symbolic teaching of art was less dramatic than that of an entire life. Despite Lanier's understanding, mildness and conciliation were not easily achieved by him. In "Remonstrance" of 1878 he ostensibly attacks science, but he shifts to an assault on the critics he berated in his lecture on Shakespeare. Those critics freed Barabbas but stabbed Christ. The poet begs: "I would thou left'st me free, to live with love."

But in "How Love Looked for Hell," written while he worked on "The Marshes of Glynn," Lanier extended the plea for freedom to an ideal description of forgiveness, and the poem recalls in its allegorical simplicity the early joust poems. Prince Love's ministers, Mind and Sense, take him to see hell; but, since hell is a matter of viewpoint, Sense insists, "I saw true hell with mine own eye"; however, Love calmly says, "But I cannot find where thou hast found/Hell." [12] At last, when Mind confesses that he had dreamed he had murdered love, Love replies with complete forgiveness, "In dreams of hate true loves begin." But the allegorical form insures that there will be no challenge to this notion of etherealization. And this problem is exactly the one which Lanier's psychological honesty has been unable to resolve in "The Marshes of Glynn."

IV *Boys' Books and Adult Essays*

Another but secondary approach by Lanier to the education of feelings was his editing of chivalric classics for boys which kept the pot boiling from 1878 to 1881. However, Lanier did use this chance to educate those who were as yet unaffected by the materialism of the Gilded Age. Apart from the customary bowdlerizing of the texts, Lanier's scholarly introductions drew ethical implications from the stories. In 1878, he wrote his publisher that *The Boy's Froissart* would direct the reader to "those persistent remains of Chivalry" in modern culture, and he notes that Chaucer, William Langland, and John Wyclif were "large and beautiful souls" to be imitated. As in his Shakespeare essays, Lanier appealed to hero worship; but he felt compelled to add that "Somehow it seems harder to be a good knight nowadays than it was then," listing the everyday problems that might tempt a boy to vice including "the utmost delicacy of national honor"—just what Lanier had called the result of uneducated feeling in his 1860 letter to his father. But Lanier was not directing his remarks solely to boys, for in *The Boy's Mabinogion* (1881) he contrasted King Arthur's love of law with contemporary legislatures which "multiply laws and murder Law." And *The Boy's King Arthur* (1880) and *The Boy's Percy* (1881) directed boys to be "fair in trade, loyal in love, generous to the poor . . . and honest in all things." He expected much from boys.

Continuing in his direct attempts to educate the public, Lanier gave a series of lectures early in 1881 about the English novel in which he argues that depth characterization is a modern innovation and in which he also summarizes and develops many ideas of his later years. He argues that the Greeks did not depict personality, or what Carlyle called "the mystery in us that calls itself *I*." Since Lanier thought everything evolved from simple to complex, from chaos to form, from definite to indefinite, he easily reconciled the theory of evolution with his idea of etherealization; but, unlike later literary Naturalists, he exempted human development from such determinism. Freedom was necessary to Lanier's moral view, and it was intimately related to his view of the ultimate synthesis of all forms that have etherealized. The growth of personality toward the Unknown, toward one's fellow man, and toward nature becomes unified by "the conception of Love as the organic idea of moral order." [13] The very form of the novel, Lanier explained, reveals a synthesis of science and poetry, as well as a spiritualization of language, for prose is a freer form than poetry because it contains more forms. The need for a freer form enabled the novel to develop from drama in order to explain "the more complex relations between modern personalities."

As Lanier had insisted that every play was a powerful sermon, so the novel is the most moral of all forms of literature; and George Eliot, because she uses a newer form and responds to modern ideas, is a more moral teacher than Shakespeare. Unlike Shakespeare, she had discovered, besides the "enormous motive of forgiveness," the mysterious forces in human personality that determine people to love each another. Because the omniscient point of view resembles, to Lanier, the omniscience of God, he calls the novel "the very highest and holiest plane of creative effort." In fact, his claims for the novel are so strong, we wonder if he might have turned to this genre again as a way to free his poetry from the technical problems he had encountered and to allow deeper explorations of human motives. His characterizations of Smallin and Cranston in *Tiger-Lilies* reveal some interest in psychological fiction.

Lanier was certainly making the most of his educational roles and used his new positions as ways to encourage the education of the feelings of his era, and he not only employed them, however indirectly, as guides to his own artistic development, but also used the opportunities to reject some of his earlier views. Only six years after writing "The Symphony" he could write that "Charity has become organic and a part of the system of things." [14] As we so often sense in Lanier's essays, his self-assurance was partly adopted to convince himself.

V *Poetic Fever*

Lanier had complained that his professional music career and his lectureships at the Peabody Institute and Johns Hopkins University made him "crush back" poems he longed to write. In 1880 he wrote: "To be an artist, and preach the gospel of poetry: that is the breath of *my* life." There was barely enough breath left for him to voice his last poems; for, since November, 1876, when a mysterious five-hundred-dollar gift had allowed him to rest in Florida, he knew he did not have long to live. Among the poems of this period is "The Crystal" (spring, 1880) in which Lanier forgives the faults of the "sweet seers and stellar visionaries" who were the greatest poets and thinkers. The poem expanded upon a letter written in November, 1876, to Bayard Taylor. He told Taylor that the greatest poets needed the greatest allowances: "What enormous artistic crimes do we have continually to pardon in Homer, Dante, Shakespeare! How often is the first utterly dull and long-winded, the second absurdly credulous and superstitious, the third over-done and fantastical!" [15]

This rather cavalier way of treating his betters occurred when Lanier was at one of the peaks of his artistic egoism. In a letter explaining this poem, Lanier stated that his use of the term "forgiveness" derived from the Lord's Prayer which demands forgiveness of those sinning against us. "It becomes thus not only our right but our duty to 'forgive' them." [16] In his zeal to forgive, Lanier had once more fallen into the Christ-like pose which robbed his work of its most interesting human insights. It is possible to argue as well that the self-satisfaction and condescension of such an attitude as that shown in "The Crystal" seriously weakened his art by allowing a relaxation into abstractions of piety when a more concrete exploration of the human condition was needed.

In "The Crystal" Lanier expands this list of writers in need of "the greatest allowances," many of whom he had listed as those ruined by capricious criticism: Buddha, Dante, Socrates, Milton, Aeschylus, Lucretius, Thomas à Kempis, Marcus Aurelius, Epictetus, Caedmon, Keats, Emerson, Langland, Emanuel Swedenborg, Jacob Behmen, Tennyson, and Shakespeare require forgiveness because they never created a perfect work of art. The only perfection ever created was Christ, and he alone needs no forgiveness. Lanier's criticism, therefore, is moral, not artistic, just as his criticism of Shakespeare had been; but he seems unwilling to make sharp distinctions between art as art and art as biographical data. Naturally, Christ alone is blameless:

> But Thee, but Thee, O Sovereign Seer of time,
> But Thee, O poets' Poet, Wisdom's Tongue,
> But Thee, O man's best Man, O love's best Love,
> O perfect life in perfect labor writ.[17]

In "The Cloud" (June, 1880) Lanier returned to the posture of social critic that he had defined years before and which he linked in his imagination to Christ, the castigator of the moneylenders. Lanier arraigns the cloud for the crimes of murder and arson and asks why it does not plunge its lightning bolts in "Some maggot politician throng/Swarming to parcel out/The body of a land, and rout/The maw-conventicle, and ungorge Wrong." [18] But Lanier forgives the cloud since it acts according to a nature designed by God. The very freedom which had so appealed to Lanier earlier now seems to be fraught with anxiety, for the artist may be free to write what he pleases, but his responsibility is great in proportion to his freedom:

> Awful is Art, because 'tis free.
> The artist trembles o'er his plan,
> Where men his Self must see.

If the language and rhythms of this poem are an indication, Lanier thought the most unadorned expression of these abstractions would be most effective. Yet the experiments of "The Symphony," "The Song of the Chattahoochee," and "The Marshes of Glynn" had shown the risks that an artist takes in trying to find his original voice. "Crystal" and "The Cloud" may suggest that Lanier had begun not only to accustom himself to a sense of the crushing responsibilities of art but also to accept the inability of man *being man* to ever succeed as an artist.

Despite his doubts, Lanier wrote two impressive poems two months before he died, "A Ballad of Trees and the Master" and

"Sunrise," which exhibit contrasting styles in the education of feeling, and two ways of living with some sense of defeat at having failed to educate nineteenth-century America, though he did his "devoirs" in obedience to the dream.

"A Ballad of Trees and the Master" is a simple, lyrically tender, and compassionate poem describing Christ's Agony in the Garden. The one person who did not need forgiveness and the model for Lanier's education of feelings, the "Poet of Poets," Christ takes the same path as the narrator of "The Marshes of Glynn":

> Into the woods my Master went,
>   Clean forspent, forspent.
> Into the woods my Master came,
>   Forspent with love and shame.
> But the olives they were not blind to Him,
> The little gray leaves were kind to Him:
> The thorn-tree had a mind to Him
>   When into the woods He came.
>
> Out of the woods my Master went,
>   And He was well content.
> Out of the woods my Master came,
>   Content with death and shame.
> When Death and Shame would woo Him last,
> From under the trees they drew Him last:
> 'Twas on a tree they slew Him—last
>   When out of the woods He came.[19]

The many repetitions of words, the rhyme links from stanza to stanza, the understated assonance, and the three-word rhymes in both stanzas carefully re-create a somber sorrow. Meanwhile, the dactyls and trochees are held in check, so that the movement does not become so quick that it distorts the tone. The poem looks back to some of Lanier's concise social protest poetry, but it is resolved, as those earlier poems are not, by the cross of salvation. And yet Lanier sees Christ in markedly human terms, enabling him to shape the personal crisis of the event. From *Tiger-Lilies* to "The Marshes of Glynn," he had shown how nature can answer man's most disturbing questions, so long as man believes that nature ultimately loves man. Yet the narrator of "The Marshes of Glynn" remained in a quandary despite his apparent willingness to believe.

Christ receives, however, the love of the garden and returns renewed to the world only to have it misunderstand and destroy him, as it was fated to do because of the deep "error" implanted in man's nature through Adam's fall. Lanier imagines that such an acceptance of the oppositions of life, such a "musical morality" (to borrow his term in analyzing Shakespeare), can only be produced by the operation of an external force, typically revealing spiritual forces. Yet the garden is odd: the olives accept Christ by negating their alternative ("were not blind to him"); and the thorn leaves have a "mind" to him. The men who will shortly put Christ through the agony of the Cross are blind to him, and they will wound his head with a crown of thorns. Though nature may be misused by man, even to being turned into a wasteland, for the moment it "has a mind" to the man who symbolizes the possibilities of spiritual regeneration. The idiom "to mind" (to "understand," "obey," or "sympathize") creates a current of understatement and suggests that the thorns, though put to a dark use, are not themselves a mysterious or hostile aspect of nature. Ironically, Christ has returned to nature at this time to prepare for death, and the chivalric language which accompanies him reminds us that he is the "great man" at last come back to the world to show it how to educate its feelings. Lanier's dark suggestion, however, is that, if such a man were to return, he would be misunderstood and killed.

"A Ballad of Trees and the Master" is such a perfect blend of Lanier's chivalric and protest themes, as well as a summation of his identification of himself with Christ and the "great man" and their probable fate, that there is little wonder he could have written it in fifteen minutes with a temperature of a hundred and four degrees. "Sunrise" was written shortly after "A Ballad of Trees and the Master"; and it offered an alternative to the artistic procedures of "A Ballad of Trees and the Master" by returning to the freer forms of the marsh poem, though it is nearly identical in theme: the preparation for death through the ministry of nature.

But Lanier's method and, surprisingly, his tone in "Sunrise," are altogether different, for the forms of dark nature are revealed without terror and with a ritualistic praise and an ecstasy of faith totally unexpected in Lanier's late poetry. "Sunrise" may have been intended, however, to continue after the "waters of sleep" had subdued the narrator of "The Marshes of Glynn":

1   In my sleep I was fain of their fellowship, fain
              Of the live-oak, the marsh, and the main.
      The little green leaves would not let me alone in my sleep;
      Up-breathed from the marshes, a message of range and of sweep,
      Interwoven with wafture of wild sea-liberties, drifting,
          Came through the lapped leaves sifting, sifting,
          Came to the gates of sleep.[20]

This time, the sweeping anapestic verse helps to reflect the growing energy of the narrator, who is almost physically pulled back to
life against his will. Or was the "sleep" actually the whole Transcendental experience of "The Marshes of Glynn"?

The link of the narrator and nature is made tenuous by the
convoluted sweep of the lines and by the understated verbals and
verbs "up-breathed," "drifting," and "sifting." Otherwise, Lanier
uses virtually the same devices of rhythm and tone color we have
examined at some length in "The Marshes of Glynn." For a moment the narrator lapses back into sleep and then his eyes open,
foreshadowing sunrise.

In the second stanza the narrator shows himself a lover of nature:

16 I have come ere the dawn, O beloved, my live-oaks, to hide
          In your gospelling glooms,—to be
      As a lover in heaven, the marsh my marsh and the sea my sea.

Not merely the major symbols but much of the imagery and language of "The Marshes of Glynn" is used from this point on. In
"gospelling glooms" Lanier recovers two images; but, in making a
metaphorical phrase of them, he gives a somewhat puritanical
overtone to the oaks, making them unlikely as a "beloved."

In the third stanza, the narrator embraces the trees with tears
that rise "not from reason." The leaves, "embroid'ring the dark of
the question of man," seem to give some "pattern and plan" to
nature; but the dark doubt of the end of "The Marshes of Glynn"
reappears: "(But would I could know, but would I could know)."
But the narrator considers himself fortunate that the leaves "have
wrought me/Designs on the night of our knowledge." He is not
content, but he is thankful for some knowledge of his mysterious
life. These lines seem to be intimately related to the problem
which ends "The Marshes of Glynn," man's inability to discover

the secrets of nature. But they are certainly not an answer. He begs nature to teach him the "terms of silence" and "the passion of patience," apparently so he can resolve his bewilderment at the ambiguous signs nature affords man. The same fears that had bothered the narrator of "The Marshes of Glynn" during his passage through the woods have also affected this narrator, but Lanier has more specifically identified these fears as crises of religious faith. Lanier supplies in "Sunrise" no transition from woods to the marsh, and he draws an image from "The Symphony" to call the marsh an "old chemist, rapt in alchymy" who has solved the secrets of matter and so distills silence. Its "precious qualities of silence" symbolize for the narrator a profound peace that cannot be his.

The next stanza of this new section brings a full tide in the marshes, but there are no puzzling forms in the water since it is dawn, not twilight. The narrator notes that the marsh outdoes the riches of heaven: the sky has but one galaxy, but the marsh has ten. This section's tone of quiet meditation has been given greater tranquility by the greater number of couplets, often heroic couplets, than in "The Marshes of Glynn." Suddenly the poem becomes agitated. The anxiety is not directed at the fear of some mysterious force in nature, however, but on behalf of the rising sun:

86   Oh, what if a sound should be made!
            Oh, what if a bound should be laid
        To this bow-and-string tension of beauty and silence a-spring,—
        To the bend of beauty the bow, or the hold of silence the string!
        I fear me, I fear me yon dome of diaphanous gleam
            Will break as a bubble o'er-blown in a dream,—
        Yon dome of too-tenuous tissues of space and of night,
            Over-weighted with stars, over-freighted with light,
            Over-sated with beauty and silence, will seem
                But a bubble that broke in a dream,
96   If a bound of degree to this grace be laid,
            Or a sound or a motion made.

As Charmenz Lenhart has rightly said, "It may seriously be doubted whether any better description of dawn with so carefully sustained a crescendo has been achieved in the English language." [21] In the thirty-seven lines leading to the sun's appearance,

Lanier has packed all the musical effects at his command; and he maintains the narrator's anxiety as the location of the excitement. Thus the enormous flood of the sun's energy is given terrific personal substance. By invoking the images of dreams to describe the tense silence before dawn, Lanier has recalled the dream of the narrator that opened the poem, with its memory of the woods, marsh, and sleep. If it has been correctly inferred that this was a dream embodying "The Marshes of Glynn," then the recollection of it at this moment dispels entirely the doubts which that dream had enclosed, as well as perhaps the worry of the ultimate questions in the woods later in that section of "Sunrise." Those worries, it now appears, may have been the aftereffects of his dreaming.

Yet motion and sound are made in the next stanza as the "wild duck sails round the bend of the river," apparently carrying the narrator's eyes eastward. Another of Lanier's spiritual birds, this one is more carefully worked into the rich tissues of detail than in any other poem. The poet becomes Whitmanesque and cosmic at this point as he momentarily springs from his own situation of almost unendurable tension to an unexpected image of a sailor seemingly hoisting the sun like a flag:

116   And a sailor unseen is hoisting a-peak,
        For list, down the inshore curve of the creek
            How merrily flutters the sail,—
        And lo, in the east! Will the East unveil?
        The East is unveiled, the East hath confessed
        A flush: 'tis dead; 'tis alive: 'tis dead, ere the West
        Was aware of it: nay, 'tis abiding, 'tis unwithdrawn:
123   Have a care, sweet Heaven! 'Tis Dawn.

The many caesuras and the unusual stress distribution produce a retarding and a quickening of the lines to create tremendous tension. Lanier's long vowels also help to slow the line, while the anapests hurry it along. This effect is especially functional in " 'Tis alive," with the caesura serving to break up the foot and thereby extend the verb's vowel beyond its usual duration. The next line puts two nonstressed syllables in succession, and a strong caesura follows to create a strange effect of hush, breaking up our sense that the foot is an anapest ("Was awáre of it: náy . . ."). This exciting segment of the poem—perhaps the most exciting in all his

poems—strains our normal expectations of patterned rhythms so
much that the "feel" of the lines is free verse.

In absolute freedom, the sun rises—a symbol of the narrator's
spiritual ascent. We recognize now that the "sunrise" the narrator
has beheld is the rising of his own soul after death, and no better
way exists to subdue a crisis of faith than to demonstrate the reality of the soul. This place would have been the perfect one for the
poem to end, but Lanier pursues the sun as it rises with an unfortunately grotesque image in which the sun is a "star-fed Bee, the
build-fire Bee" returning to a "hive" of the sky, the "gold undaz-
zling" zenith. Heroic couplets restore the peaceful scene to its
former tranquility in the next stanza in which the marsh worships
the sun by reflecting it. The following stanza draws the major
symbols together with the poet's soul in a way that resembles
Whitman's "symphonic" form:

149   With several voice, with ascription one,
       The woods and the marsh and the sea and my soul
    Unto thee, whence the glittering stream of all morrows doth roll,
    Cry good and past-good and most heavenly morrow, lord Sun.

In the last section of "Sunrise" Lanier reaches back to "Corn"
for the highest praise of the sun: "Yea, Artist, thou, of whose art
yon sea's all news,/With his inshore greens and manifold mid-sea
blues." But "Corn" appears, in contrast, amateurish; for the sun is
the source for all nature's energy, not merely an exemplar of it; it
gives the marshes their form and color, and it makes clear what is
mysterious in all forms of nature. The narrator can therefore return to the dailiness of life with a regenerated heart: "strong with
the strength of my lord the Sun:/How dark, how dark soever the
race that must needs be run,/I am lit with the Sun."

We feel that Lanier has at last written in "Sunrise" a mystical
poem, the kind of poetry his musicality of verse was best suited
for and which his essentially religious concepts of the synthesis of
the arts could make most provocative. The impressionistic technique following the lead, sometimes too automatically, of "The
Marshes of Glynn," is welded to a triangular form in which the
poem reaches its apex as the sun does, and it falls smoothly away
into a retrenched belief in life. But the poem is given internal
solidity through its inclusion of the traditions of chivalry, on the

one hand, which always settled oppositions through religous para-doxes, and protest, on the other, which brought Lanier to recog-nize the sometimes irreconcilable injustices of life, some of which he came to regard as not circumstantial but as existential.

The sun is a symbol of pure feeling, and it is offered to the world as a potential symbol for all men. The final exemplar, it is the last demonstration of the reason for responding first to feeling rather than to thought. Only through an onomatopoetic represen-tation of the effect of the sun on a poet's soul can the poet con-vince his audience that his age has not truly been alive. The river with its song of duty and the woods, marsh, sea, and sunrise are evoked by Lanier's rich musicality in such a way that we must feel our way toward the essence of the natural objects he represents. Thus, his music liberates us from the images which we may dis-cover to be turgid, confused, obscure, trite, or sentimental. By freeing us from semantic responses insofar as he is able, Lanier invites a direct participation in the musical language.

CHAPTER 8

Conclusion

GROUNDED in a conservative literary society in the South, one made the more recessive by a "tragic era," Lanier could not dispense with the weaker elements of that literary heritage: sentimentality, didacticism, a trite assortment of themes and subjects, and a sententious and abstract rhetoric. Yet he looked forward with the literary and musical vanguard of his nation to newer forms that could liberate the ineffective mannerisms of an artificial art. His life work shows a circuitous route to the discovery of his forms and procedures, but it also shows that he could not break with older forms or open himself entirely to the implications of newer ones. Perhaps the crisis of soul delineated in "The Marshes of Glynn," "A Ballad of Trees and the Master," and "Sunrise" suggests why Lanier could never commit himself to Whitman's free verse or to Swinburne's pre-Symbolist "esthetic poetry." Temperamentally and artistically, Lanier did not have the total dedication needed to distill the reversals of his life or the indifference of his age. Yet he persisted in following his own inner gleam —in the end, he found his unique poetic voice, and American literature has found a place for him not because his art is eccentric or because he wrote during the literary doldrums but because his finest work has the integrity of craft, unusual insight, and some philosophical density.

But it is not sufficient to leave Lanier with a review of his aims and achievements. A few questions about his place in American and Southern literature remain because of the unfair reception accorded him by leading Southern writers, particularly by those who are credited with having founded the Southern Renaissance through their editing of the *Fugitive* in the 1920's, John Crowe Ransom, Allen Tate, and Robert Penn Warren. Warren, in his review of Aubrey Starke's biography of Lanier, is determined to refute Starke's claim that Lanier was a precursor of the Southern

Renaissance: "He was the final product of all that was dangerous in Romanticism: his theory of personality, his delusion of prophecy, his aesthetic premise, his uninformed admiration of science, his nationalism, his passion for synthesis, his theory of progress. What was valuable in his century passed him by. He was admired because, as Tennyson to England, he spoke to America, and tardily to the South, in the accent of its dearest anticipations." [1]

Warren's hasty generalizations need individual consideration. As for Lanier's "theory of personality," he presented in *The English Novel* one of the few American comments of his time that foresaw the rise of psychological fiction. The "delusion of prophecy" was one he shared with William Blake, Walt Whitman, W. B. Yeats, and Warren himself in *Brothers to Dragons;* and Lanier adopted the pose of poet-prophet as his way of insisting upon the seriousness of his calling at a time when "parlor poetry" was called art. If Lanier's "aesthetic premise"—the relation of music to poetry?—damaged him as a poet, it also liberated him from the conventions of his fellow poets and provided him with a unique poetic contribution which Warren has never carefully examined. Lanier's "admiration of science" was hardly uninformed, as Gay W. Allen has shown; had he been ignorant as charged, would we accuse him for not condemning science because it became in our time the servant of the military-industrial complex? As for Lanier's "nationalism" (inferred exclusively from "The Centennial Meditation" and "The Psalm of the West"), neither Warren, Tate, nor Ransom observe that those poems do not reverse Lanier's social protest of 1867–68; instead, Lanier emphasizes the theme of spiritual progress in those admittedly inferior occasional poems. He praised Christopher Columbus, not Ulysses S. Grant. Could anyone criticize a dying poet for accepting these commissions? Lanier did insist that he would overthrow the "culture poets" once he had infiltrated the poetry establishment. Van Wyck Brooks has shown that the nineteenth-century American writer could do little else. Though Warren accuses Lanier of missing the "valuable" in his time, Warren does not identify what was "valuable," though he benefits by hindsight. Lanier, however, spent his life trying to clarify the religious, artistic, and philosophical ideas which he saw endangered. Can "value" ever be more than subjective?

If Warren is nonetheless accurate in asserting that Lanier "appreciated a work of art to the degree in which it supported his especial theory of progress," he does not prove that this injured Lanier's poetry. A close reading of the marsh poems would have shown Warren that Lanier was hardly following the prevailing taste for progress, synthesis, and optimism; though these appear in his work as factors in his personal artistic consciousness. Though the Fugitive-Agrarians of twentieth-century America could see the dangers of progress and denounce them in their manifesto, *I'll Take My Stand,* what could a sensitive, isolated, tubercular Southern poet do in the late nineteenth century besides hope for the future and trace the paths open to private regeneration?

Though Tate and Warren have gone to some trouble to show that "The Psalm of the West" is an inferior poem, they did their own critical talents a disservice by comparing Lanier's weakest poems to those of Donne and Marvell. Cleanth Brooks and Warren published a biting attack on "My Springs" in *Understanding Poetry* (1938)—the most influential critical anthology of our time —but mainly to promote their own theories of poetry. Nonetheless, they permit to stand as criticism of Lanier's total poetic output an attack of a poem so minor that it has been included in only three of one hundred and fifty anthologies presenting Lanier's work.

Certainly, next to Timrod, Hayne, Taylor, Fathers Tabb and Ryan, and even Whitman, Lanier's aggressive imagination, his musical sensitivity, and his ability to transform commonplace symbols into Transcendental experiences make a distinct force in and contribution to nineteenth-century American poetry. Against personal hazards, Lanier sought to impose his voice on an age that had beaten Melville, discarded Whitman, debased Emerson, co-opted Twain, and walled in Emily Dickinson.

Lanier's defects of intellect and ability are frequently, as in any writer, a test of a critic's patience. It is not unusual for a commentator to develop condescension toward a writer because he perceives his flaws so much more clearly than the writer could. But the question John Gould Fletcher raised remains: despite his flaws, how good was Lanier at his best? As I have tried to show, Lanier was a writer capable of unexpected brilliance and of special moments of excitement and beauty. His adherence to feeling shows a remarkable case of an artist's attempt to model reality on his concept. Facing contradictions and misfortunes, he was in many ways courageous in his determination to write what his heart demanded; and he was quite original in his distillation of experience into poetry. Lanier constructed a world view from the things he had learned in college and shortly thereafter, and he measured every later experience by them, sometimes to his disadvantage.

Lanier's creative compulsions have helped to form the modern tradition in poetry which derives from Baudelaire, Rimbaud, Verlaine, Mallarmé, and other French poets and which had been presaged by Poe and the English Romantic poets Coleridge, Shelley, and Keats. Lanier's contemporaries, Whitman, Tennyson, Swinburne, and Dante Rossetti, also shared some similarities with Symbolist poets. All were concerned with turning poetry toward more serious aims than either didactic sentiment or the personal effusions of sensitive plants. In his attempt to exploit the musicality of verse, Lanier certainly deserves a place with these writers. As I have suggested, it is unfortunate that he lacked the confidence to pursue his aims to their conclusions, as Mallarmé did in constructing a poetry that is sometimes sensible only as music. Mme. Therese Bentzon in 1898 recognized affinities between Lanier, the "musical poet," and the *Symbolistes,* the French group whose members have been named above; and one American expatriate attached to the group, "Le Goffic," translated Lanier's "Life and Song" into French.

If Lanier's adherence to feeling were a retreat from reality, as it has been charged, he typified in this respect the South's need for psychological withdrawal and spiritual consolidation as it absorbed the nature of defeat. Lanier in a way began what some have called the "reconstruction of Southern literature" by his articulation of a belief in emotion that has become the dominant pattern of Southern literature. We cannot resist the inference that Tate, Warren, and, to a lesser extent, Ransom had to reject Lanier —even though his ideas of agrarian reform in "The New South" (1880) were much like their advocations in *I'll Take My Stand*—[2] because he was identified with the magnolia-moonbeams-mint-julep clichés of the antebellum South. As Ransom wrote in the first issue of the *Fugitive* in 1922, "We flee from nothing faster than the high-caste Brahmins of the old South."

This view was unfortunate, because the poised ironies with which Ransom balances feeling against intellect, like the oppositions of men of thought and men of action in Warren's novels, ultimately derive part of their cultural origin from Lanier's oppositions of heart and mind. From James Branch Cabell's fantasies to William Faulkner's novels of the naked endurance of primitives who distrust intellect, we sense the continuous allegiance to feeling represented in and by Lanier. Virtually any Southern writer can be included in those dealing with this opposition of feeling and thought—James Agee, Truman Capote, Carson McCullers, Erskine Caldwell, Flannery O'Connor, Eudora Welty, Conrad Aiken, Allen Tate, Andrew Lytle, Randall Jarrell, William Styron, and Tennessee Williams, to name the most prominent ones. Of course the conflict of heart and head is not exclusively Southern: Hawthorne and Melville used it extensively. Yet the intense concern over moral feeling in Southern literature radiates a special tone when it is considered as a total body of work. And, since this tradition has been responsible for much of the best writing in our century, acknowledgment should be directed to Lanier. He was instrumental to the development of American literature.

Notes and References

Preface

1. John Gould Fletcher, "Sidney Lanier," *University of Kansas City Review*, XX (Winter, 1949), 97.

2. Allen Tate, "A Southern Romantic," *New Republic*, LXXVI (August 30, 1933), 67.

Chapter One

1. Charles R. Anderson and Aubrey Starke, *The Centennial Edition of the Works of Sidney Lanier* (Baltimore, 1945), VII, 33. Referred to afterward as *Centennial Edition*.

2. Untitled, unpublished essay, c. 1860, p. 2.

3. Untitled, unpublished essay, c. 1859, p. 5.

4. Sir James MacIntosh, *Dissertation on the Progress of Ethical Philosophy* (Edinburgh, 1862), p. 258.

5. "Virtue—How Distinguished from Piety," unpublished essay, c. 1860, p. 2. Lanier relied, possibly, on the similar survey of moral philosophy in an unsigned review of Paley's work, "The Works of William Paley," in *Southern Quarterly Review*, XXIX (April, 1856), 118–50.

6. "Is Happiness ever a Legitimate Object of Pursuit?" unpublished essay, c. 1860, p. 4.

7. "Second Speech Peroration," unpublished essay, c. 1860, p. 1.

8. "Desire and Thought," unpublished essay, p. 82. This is the first draft of the essay which was to become "The Error of Cousin and Hamilton." It was probably written in 1868, occupying pages 68–100 of a "small volume" of essays. "Desire and Thought" was a revision of "The Oversight of Modern Philosophy" (c. 1867–69) which appeared in Lanier's Ledger, pp. 238–41 and 282–84. My conjectural dating is based on the place of the essay in the Ledger. Lanier's view of Hamilton may have derived from the unsigned essay, "The Infinite," in *Southern Quarterly Review*, XXIX (August, 1856), 294–312.

9. In a short note written in winter, 1881, Lanier wrote: "the more we know, the more we know that we don't know. Wm Hamilton's knowledge is the consummation of human ignorance." (Quoted in

Charles Anderson, "Lanier and Science: Addenda," *Modern Language Notes,* LXVI [June, 1951], 395–98.)

10. Thomas Carlyle, *Critical and Miscellaneous Essays* (1846 and 1858), p. 78. These editions are identical and evidence from Lanier's letters firmly shows he read this volume. See *Centennial Edition,* VII, 117, as well as evidence in Chapter 2. Carlyle's "Signs of the Times" might have been a source for some of Lanier's thoughts on the direction of modern philosophy.

11. "The Error of Cousin and Hamilton," p. 99.

Chapter Two

1. *Centennial Edition,* V. 5.

2. The quotations from and paraphrases of Goethe come directly from Carlyle's essays on Goethe. Lanier used in particular "Goethe's Helena," but he probably read all six of Carlyle's essays on Goethe in this volume (see note 10, Chapter 1) as well as the other eleven essays on German writing included in it.

3. William Baskervill, *Southern Writers* (Nashville, 1897), p. 155.

4. *Centennial Edition,* VII, 57.

5. Regarding Novalis, Lanier made eight separate uses of him, all of which can be traced to Carlyle's "Novalis" in his *Critical and Miscellaneous Essays.* (See note 10, Chapter 1.) Lanier quoted Richter fourteen times and all except one derive from Carlyle's two essays on Richter in the above volume. Apparently, Lanier did read a translation of Richter's *Flower, Fruit, and Thorn Pieces,* since he used a quotation from it as an epigraph in *Tiger-Lilies.* (*Centennial Edition,* V, 52.)

6. Jack De Bellis, "Sidney Lanier and German Romance: An Important Qualification," *Comparative Literature Studies,* V (June, 1968), 145–57. Even Edmund Wilson was misguided by faulty scholarship in *Patriotic Gore* (1962).

7. *Centennial Edition,* VIII, 31.

8. *Ibid.,* V, 38.

9. *Ibid.,* 37.

10. Carlyle, pp. 59–60.

11. *Ibid.,* p. 61.

12. *Centennial Edition,* VII, 243.

13. "Retrospects and Prospects," unpublished, undated essay, p. 47. This is the second draft of the essay and was written about May, 1867. The final draft appears in *Centennial Edition,* V, 280–305. (For dating of this manuscript, see *Centennial Edition,* V, 280n.)

14. "The New Time," unpublished and undated essay, pp. 15–16. This is probably the first draft of "Retrospects and Prospects," written about March 22, 1867.

15. Thomas Carlyle, *Sartor Resartus, On Heroes and Hero Worship* (London, 1959), p. 317.

16. *Centennial Edition*, V, 12.

17. *Ibid.*, 162–63.

18. *Ibid.*, 139.

Chapter Three

1. Edd Winfield Parks, *Ante-Bellum Southern Literary Critics* (Athens, 1962), p. 109.

2. John Crowe Ransom, ed., *I'll Take My Stand* (New York: 1930). See especially Ransom's Introduction and his chapter, "Reconstructed but Unregenerate."

3. In Lanier's library with 1856 dates are these Waverley novels of Scott: *Guy Mannering, The Antiquary, Rob Roy, The Pirates,* and *The Heart of Mid-Lothian.*

4. H. J. Eckenrode, "Sir Walter Scott and the South," *North American Review*, CCVI (October, 1917), 595–603. His position derives from Twain's and has been severely questioned by G. Harrison Orians, "Walter Scott, Mark Twain and the Civil War," *South Atlantic Quarterly*, XL (October, 1941), 344–48. Orians argues that Scott was as popular in the North and West as in the South, that his influence was indirect, and that he was no more significant than Carlyle in creating Southern character.

5. For additional comments by Mark Twain, see *Life on the Mississippi*, Chapters 40, 45, and 46.

6. *Centennial Edition*, IV, 159.

7. Bruce Catton, *A Stillness at Appomattox* (New York, 1958), p. 21.

8. Willard Thorp, ed., *A Southern Reader* (New York, 1955), pp. 261–62.

9. *Centennial Edition*, VII, 134. Rolin G. Osterweis, *Romanticism and Nationalism in the Old South* (New Haven, 1949), pp. 4–5, lists a tournament held September 2, 1845, featuring the "Knight of La Mancha." For one who fled from sentimental traditions so much, Allen Tate gives a surprisingly graphic, insightful account of an antebellum tournament in *The Fathers* (Denver, 1960), pp. 40–79.

10. *Ibid.*, X, 139n. As late as 1971 tournaments were being held in Virginia.

11. Willard Thorp, p. 260.

12. *Centennial Edition*, V, 272.

13. W. J. Cash, *The Mind of the South* (New York, 1960), p. 89.

14. Clifford Lanier, "Reminiscences of Sidney Lanier," *Chautauquan*, XXI (July, 1895), 404.

15. *Centennial Edition*, V, 274.

16. George Herbert Clarke, *Some Reminiscences and Early Letters of Sidney Lanier* (Macon, 1907), p. 14.

17. *Centennial Edition,* VII, 171.

18. Thomas Wentworth Higginson, *Contemporaries* (New York, 1899), p. 101.

19. *Centennial Edition,* VII, 125, 286.

20. *Ibid.,* 376.

21. *Ibid.,* IX, 239.

22. Philip Graham, "Sidney Lanier and the Pattern of Contrast," *American Quarterly,* IX (Winter, 1959), 506.

23. Ledger, unpublished, conjecturally dated c. 1865, p. 2.

24. *Centennial Edition,* I, 6.

25. *Ibid.,* 6–8. A quantifying survey of Lanier's archaisms is Clark Olney's, "Archaisms in the Poetry of Sidney Lanier," *Notes and Queries,* CLXVI (April 28, 1934), 292–94.

26. See *ibid.,* VII, 126, 131, 136, and 141.

27. Robert Penn Warren, "The Blind Poet: Sidney Lanier," *American Review,* II (November, 1933), 27. See also Allen Tate, "A Southern Romantic," *New Republic,* LXXVI (August 30, 1933), 67–70.

28. *Centennial Edition,* V, 291.

29. *Ibid.,* VII, 397.

30. Sir Walter Scott, "An Essay on Chivalry," *The Complete Works of Sir Walter Scott* (Philadelphia, 1857), p. 4.

31. F. J. C. Hearnshaw, "Chivalry and Its Place in History," *Chivalry,* Edgar Prestage, ed. (New York, 1928), p. 30.

32. *Centennial Edition,* I, 171–89.

33. Darrell Abel, *American Literature,* II (Woodbury, 1963), 509. *Centennial Edition,* VIII, 224. Lanier wrote: "You know what the commercial spirit is: you remember that Trade killed Chivalry and now sits in the throne. It was Trade that hatched the Jacquerie in the 14th Century: it was Trade that hatched John Brown, and broke the saintly heart of Robert Lee, in the 19th."

Chapter Four

1. E. Merton Coulter, *The South During Reconstruction* (Baton Rouge, 1947), p. 2.

2. *Centennial Edition,* V, 200–203.

3. *Ibid.,* 204–5.

4. *Ibid.,* VII, 229.

5. *Ibid.,* V, 209–12.

6. *Ibid.,* VII, 270, 72.

7. *Ibid.,* V, 280–305.

8. *Ibid.,* VII, 279.

9. *Ibid.,* I, 166, 326. Aubrey Starke quotes several lines from this

poem in *Sidney Lanier*, p. 113, but says nothing of their ultimate excision.

10. *Ibid.*, VII, 346.

11. *Ibid.*, 373n.

12. *Ibid.*, I, 13–14.

13. *Ibid.*, 14.

14. *Ibid.*, 15.

15. *Ibid.*, 288. In Anderson's opinion, "Raven's Food" is an expansion of "Raven Days," written "subsequent to the shorter version (which Lanier himself selected for publication), but rejected because of its bitterness." Anderson mentions an earlier draft of the "shorter version" ("Raven Days") dated February 25, 1868. It seems a moot point whether the long poem was an expansion of the shorter, or the shorter an extraction from the longer. But it seems likely Lanier must have actually added the stanzas making "Raven's Food" after his crisis had passed.

16. *Ibid.*, V, 231–46.

17. *Ibid.*, VII, 392.

18. *Ibid.*, V, 306–21.

19. *Ibid.*, VII, 400n.

20. *Ibid.*, VIII, 79.

21. *Ibid.*, V, 247–64. J. W. De Forest presented a similar contrast between North and South one month later: "The civilisation of the South is defective, doubtless, but it is a civilisation seeking a spiritual elevation over matter and money." ("Chivalrous Southrons," *Southern Review*, XI (July, 1869), 110.

22. *Ibid.*, VIII, 11.

23. *Ibid.*, I, 22–23. Considerable confusion shrouds the composition of this poem. The 1884 edition of Lanier's poetry notes it was published "in a Georgia Daily, 1869," but the earliest reference to it in Lanier's letters was March 11 (?), 1871. It was published first on February 7, 1871, and no search of the Georgia magazines has revealed any previous publication.

24. *Ibid.*, 191–94. Claude Bowers' *Tragic Era* has described the Ku-Klux Act as a measure which "set aside the constitutional guarantees of the States as effectively as though they had never been written" (p. 342).

25. *Ibid.*, 24–25.

26. *Ibid.*, 194–96. The title seems to derive from Lewis Carroll's *Through the Looking-Glass*. In chapter nine the Red Queen demands that Alice "take nine from eight." Alice sensibly replies, "Nine from eight I can't, you know."

27. *Ibid.*, xxxiv.

28. *Ibid.*, V, 266–67.

29. *Ibid.*, I, 41.

30. *Ibid.*, 42.

31. *Ibid.*, VIII, 224.

32. *Ibid.*, IX, 121–22.

33. *Ibid.*, I, 293.

34. *Ibid.*, 34–39.

35. *Ibid.*, IX, 96. E. P. Kuhl, "Sidney Lanier and Edward Spencer," *Studies in Philology*, XXVII (July, 1930), 470, has identified W. D. Howells' taste for bird poems as the source of his "editorial blunder." Howells had printed several poems by Paul Hamilton Hayne. See also Aubrey Starke's "William Dean Howells and Sidney Lanier," *American Literature*, III (March, 1931), 79–82.

Chapter Five

1. *Centennial Edition*, VIII, 347.

2. *Ibid.*, 330.

3. *Ibid.*, 419.

4. *Ibid.*, 99. See also "Retrospects and Prospects": "This is the art of to-day . . . into whose hands has fallen the unfinished work of the bygone arts" (*ibid.*, V, 290).

5. *Ibid.*, IX, 3.

6. *Ibid.*, VIII, 335.

7. *Ibid.*, VI, 389–90; X, 290.

8. Sidney Lanier, "Infinite Solecisms," unpublished essay, c. 1869, p. 409. A strikingly similar idea occurs in Carlyle's "The Opera": "Music is well said to be the speech of angels. . . . It brings us near to the Infinite." (Thomas Carlyle, *Critical and Miscellaneous Essays*, II [Boston, 1885], 340.)

9. *Centennial Edition*, IX, 101.

10. *Ibid.*, VI, 161.

11. *Ibid.*, IX, 334, 335n.

12. *Ibid.*, 39–40.

13. Cleanth Brooks and Robert Penn Warren, *Understanding Poetry* (New York, 1966), pp. 301–2.

14. Philip Graham, "A Note on Lanier's Music," *Studies in English* (University of Texas), XVII (1937), 107–11.

15. Richard Webb, "Sidney Lanier, Poet and Prosodist," *Sidney Lanier, Poet and Prosodist*, Richard Webb and Edwin R. Coulson, eds. (Athens, 1941), p. 47.

16. *Centennial Edition*, I, 42–43.

17. Thomas Carlyle, "The Hero as Poet," pp. 316–17.

18. *Centennial Edition*, IX, 319. Though he wrote on October 30, 1869, "A healthful, noble, picturesque poet is this Wm Morris! How *Keats* would have loved him!!", by August, 1875, Lanier found these

poetic models replacing his youthful idols: "No, Tennyson and William Morris are not the masters. . . . Chaucer and Shakespeare—these are the Masters" (*ibid.*, 233). This marks the start of Lanier's growth toward originality.

19. *Ibid.*, 182.

20. *Ibid.*, V, 291.

21. *Ibid.*, IX, 49–50.

22. *Ibid.*, VIII, 431.

23. Robert Penn Warren, "The Blind Poet: Sidney Lanier," *American Review*, II (November, 1933), 38.

24. Aubrey Starke, *Sidney Lanier*, pp. 209–10.

25. Richard Webb, p. 67.

26. Gay W. Allen, p. 290.

27. Charmenz Lenhart, p. 256.

28. *Centennial Edition*, I, 46–56.

29. Paul Fussell, Jr., *Poetic Meter and Poetic Form* (New York, 1965), p. 116.

30. Kenneth Burke, *The Philosophy of Literary Form*, "On Musicality in Verse" (New York, 1957), pp. 296–98.

31. Lanier included the same idea in "Retrospects and Prospects," when he wrote that Nature had risen half way to the "Spirit of man" through the Greeks' use of myth, but the modern poets "have flown out and put a star on the forehead of each rock and tree and cloud and wave; it is the star of love and grief which is worn by purified man" (*Centennial Edition*, V, 286). Anderson has suggested that etherealization declined in importance to Lanier, though it is all-pervasive and takes many forms. (Charles Anderson, "Lanier and Science: Addenda," *Modern Language Notes*, LXVI [June, 1951], 395–98.)

32. *Centennial Edition*, V, 296.

33. *Ibid.*, IX, 186.

34. John Crowe Ransom, 557–58.

35. *Centennial Edition*, IX, 205.

36. Mary Day Lanier, *Letters of Sidney Lanier* (New York, 1907), p. 113. This letter is in Mary Day Lanier's handwriting and was not printed in the *Centennial Edition* by Anderson and Starke, though it had been included in the file of letters for 1875 which those editors had compiled. Anderson has suggested privately that it may not have been included because one of the editors had doubted its authenticity or because its substance had been given more fully in another letter. Yet no comment quite like it exists in any other letters.

Chapter Six

1. *Centennial Edition*, IX, 289n.

2. *Ibid.*, I, 60–62.

3. *Ibid.*, IX, 302.

4. *Ibid.*, I, 303.

5. *Ibid.*, IX, 316–17.

6. *Ibid.*, III, 97.

7. *Ibid.*, I, 62–82.

8. John Crowe Ransom, 561.

9. Roy Harvey Pearce, *The Continuity of American Poetry* (Princeton, 1961), 236–46.

10. Robert Penn Warren, 35.

11. Frederick Conner, *Cosmic Optimism* (Gainesville, 1949), p. 210.

12. Allen Tate, "A Southern Romantic," 70.

13. *Centennial Edition*, IX, 356.

14. *Ibid.*, 369.

15. *Ibid.*

16. *Ibid.*, 374.

17. *Ibid.*, I, 103–4.

18. It is difficult to understand Lenhart's comments: "Most of the inherent musicality does not stem from repetitive consonants or rhyme or alliteration; it is not, in short, melodious—but it has a structure that is repetitive, impetuous, and ideally suited to the subject" (Lenhart, p. 269).

19. *Centennial Edition*, IX, 443.

20. *Ibid.*, 446.

21. *Ibid.*, I, 96.

22. *Ibid.*, IV, 235.

23. *Ibid.*, IX, 153.

24. *Ibid.*, X, 18.

25. *Ibid.*, 40.

26. *Ibid.*, IV, 54.

27. *Ibid.*, II, 323.

28. *Ibid.*, 326–27.

29. *Ibid.*, I, 119–22.

30. Harry Warfel, "Mystic Vision in 'The Marshes of Glynn'," *Mississippi Quarterly*, XIX (Winter, 1965–66), 34–40.

31. Robert H. Ross, "The Marshes of Glynn: A Study in Symbolic Obscurity," *American Literature*, XXXII (January, 1961), 403–17.

32. *Centennial Edition*, V, 27.

33. *Ibid.*, 88.

34. *Ibid.*, VIII, 225.

35. *Ibid.*, II, 327.

36. *Ibid.*, I, 284.

Chapter Seven

1. Aubrey Starke, *Sidney Lanier,* pp. 316, 498, note 29.
2. The impact of Swinburne may be quickly summarized. In 1866 Lanier transcribed one of his poems in a letter, suggesting one of his own was the less obscure. (*Centennial Edition,* VII, 251.) In 1868 he revealed that he thought Swinburne had a foul imagination though an excellent technique (VII, 395). In "Retrospects and Prospects" of 1868, Lanier said: "Swinburne has overheard some sea-conversation which he has translated into good English" (V, 286). By 1870 Lanier had found Swinburne had given in to public acclaim and deserted serious poetry (VIII, 79). After that Swinburne became the symbol of "culture poets" (IX, 298). In the same year Swinburne apparently weighed Lanier's poetry and disliked it (*ibid.,* note). Yet Lanier bought his *Atalanta in Calydon* (which was far inferior to *Leaves of Grass* in Lanier's private estimation). (X, 18.) He requested Swinburne's *Studies in Shakespeare* (X, 169) in 1880. A late poem outline is judicious and pungent: "He invited me to eat, the service was silver and gold, but no food therein save pepper and salt" (I, 260).
3. Karl Shapiro, *A Bibliography of Modern Prosody* (Baltimore, 1948), p. 16.
4. Joseph W. Hendren, "Time and Stress in English Verse, with Special Reference to Lanier's Theory of Rhythm," *Rice Institute Pamphlet,* XLVI (July, 1959), v–vii, 1–72.
5. Paul Fussell, Jr., p. 21.
6. Allen Tate, "A Southern Romantic," 67.
7. Joseph W. Hendren, p. 2.
8. *Centennial Edition,* II, 194–95.
9. *Ibid.,* III, 186.
10. *Ibid.,* 360.
11. *Ibid.,* 410.
12. *Ibid.,* I, 125–27.
13. *Ibid.,* IV, 145.
14. *Ibid.,* 107. In "The New South" Lanier could even assert that with slavery abolished Negroes were accepted for their true selves (V, 344, 345n.).
15. *Ibid.,* IX, 413.
16. *Ibid.,* X, 224.
17. *Ibid.,* I, 138.
18. *Ibid.,* 140.
19. *Ibid.,* 144.
20. *Ibid.,* 144–49.
21. Charmenz Lenhart, pp. 278–79.

Chapter Eight

1. Robert Penn Warren, 45.
2. *Centennial Edition*, V, 334–58. Sections of "The New South" could have appeared in those "Tracts Against Communism" as the essays that formed *I'll Take My Stand* were to be called. See especially pp. 338–39.

Selected Bibliography

PRIMARY SOURCES

1. Published Works

ANDERSON, CHARLES R., ed. *Centennial Edition of the Works of Sidney Lanier*. Baltimore: Johns Hopkins Press, 1945. Ten Volumes. Associate editors and contents of each volume are as follows: I. *Poems*, Charles Anderson sole editor; II. *The Science of English Verse and Essays on Music*, Paull F. Baum; III. *Shakespeare and his Forerunners*, Kemp Malone; IV. *The English Novel and Essays on Literature*, Clarence Gohdes and Kemp Malone; V. *Tiger-Lilies and Southern Prose*, Garland Greever; VI. *Florida and Miscellaneous Prose*, Philip Graham; VII–X. *Letters*, Charles Anderson and Aubrey Starke.

Poem Outlines. Lanier, Henry W., ed. New York: Scribner's Sons, 1908.

Letters of Sidney Lanier. Lanier, Mary Day, ed. New York: Scribner's Sons, 1907.

2. Manuscripts

"Desire and Thought." 20 pages. In Lanier's Ledger, pp. 74–93; c. spring, 1866.

"The Error of Cousin and Hamilton." 32 pages. c. 1868.

"Infinite Solecisms." 28 pages. In Lanier's Ledger, pp. 384–409. c. 1869.

"Is the Assassination of Tyrants Ever Justifiable?" 10 pages. c. 1860.

Ledger. 572 pages. c. 1860–69.

"The New Time." 28 pages. c. March, 1867.

"The Oversight of Modern Philosophy." 7 pages. In Lanier's Ledger, pp. 238–41, 282–84. c. 1867–68.

"Pursuit of Happiness." 3 pages. c. 1860.

"Pursuit of Happiness: Second Speech Peroration." 11 pages. c. 1860.

"Retrospects and Prospects." 91 pages. c. May, 1867.

"To What Are the Involuntary States of Mind Responsible?" 16 pages. c. 1860.

Untitled Speech before the Thalians. 2 pages. c. 1860.
"Virtue—How Distinguished from Piety?" 10 pages. c. 1860. (These manuscripts are in the Charles D. Lanier collection, Johns Hopkins University.)

SECONDARY SOURCES

ABEL, DARRELL. "Sidney Lanier." *American Literature.* Vol. II. Woodbury, New York, 1963. Perceptive, unpretentious introduction.
ANDERSON, CHARLES R., ed. *Centennial Edition of the Works of Sidney Lanier.* Baltimore: Johns Hopkins Press, 1945. The introductions in these ten volumes form the best critical writing available on Lanier, particularly the essays by Anderson and Baum. Weed the bibliography carefully.
GRAHAM, PHILIP. "Sidney Lanier and the Pattern of Contrast," *American Quarterly,* XI (Winter, 1956), 54–56. Tracing of an important pattern in Lanier's thought, comprehensively and comparatively.
HENDREN, JOSEPH W. *Time and Stress in English Verse, with Special Reference to Lanier's Theory of Rhythm.* Rice Institute Pamphlets, XLVI (July, 1959), v–vii and 1–72. As Chapter 7 showed, this essay rescues Lanier's scansion theory and places his most important ideas in an informed, intelligent context.
MILES, DUDLEY. "The New South: Lanier." *The Cambridge History of American Literature.* Allen Peterfield Trent, Carl Van Doren, John Erskine, and Stuart P. Sherman eds. New York: Macmillan Co., 1936. Authoritative, though dated, historical approach to Lanier's importance.
PEARCE, ROY HARVEY. *The Continuity of American Poetry.* Princeton: Princeton University Press, 1961. Best single essay on Lanier's work; also the most serious evaluation of his social and philosophical situation.
RANSOM, JOHN CROWE. "Hearts and Heads," *American Review,* II (March, 1934), 554–71. Adjudication of the conflicting claims of Robert Penn Warren and Aubrey Starke for Lanier's relevance to modern Southern culture.
ROSS, ROBERT. "The Marshes of Glynn: Study in Symbolic Obscurity," *American Literature,* XXXII (January, 1961), 403–16. Presents a good but unsuccessful attack upon Lanier as a poet.
STARKE, AUBREY. *Sidney Lanier.* Chapel Hill: University of North Carolina Press, 1933. Definitive biography of Lanier but marred by poor readings of the poetry.
TATE, ALLEN. "A Southern Romantic," *New Republic,* LXXVI (August 30, 1933), 67–70. Blistering attack on Starke's conclusions which found Lanier a precursor of the Fugitive Agrarian writers like

Tate who developed the Southern Renaissance. Useful as an evaluation of Lanier's poetry against the best poetry.

WARREN, ROBERT PENN. "The Blind Poet: Sidney Lanier," *American Review*, II (November, 1933), 27–45. Iconoclastic attack by a major poet-critic on Starke, particularly the esthetic theories that had helped create Lanier's weaknesses as a poet.

WILLIAMS, STANLEY T. "Experiments in Poetry: Sidney Lanier and Emily Dickinson." *A Literary History of the United States*. Robert Spiller, Willard Thorp, Thomas Johnson, and Henry Canby, eds. New York: Macmillan Co., 1948. Useful scholarly assessment of Lanier, particularly of the effect of his musical theories on his verse.

Index

Abel, Darrell, 45
Aeschylus, 137
Agee, James, 150
Aiken, Conrad, 150
Allen, Gay Wilson, 81, 82
American Prosody (Gay Wilson Allen), 81
Anderson, Charles R., 46, 59, 111

Bach, Johann Sebastian, 73
Baltimore Bulletin, 98
Baudelaire, Charles, 132, 149
Beethoven, Ludwig van, 71, 72, 104, 113
Behmen, Jacob, 137
Bentzon, Mme. Therese, 149
Berlioz, Hector, 70, 71, 72, 74, 104
Biglow, Hosea, 60
Blake, William, 147
Bleckley, Logan, 61, 64, 65
Breckenridge, John C., 51
Brooks, Cleanth, 75, 148
Brooks, Van Wyck, 147
Brother to Dragons (Robert Penn Warren), 147
Brown in "9 from 8," 57
Browning, Robert, 43, 76, 81
Bryant, William Cullen, 75, 119
Buck, Dudley, 98, 99
Buddha, 137
Burke, Kenneth, 82, 83, 87, 95
Butler, Samuel, 55

Cabell, James Branch, 150
Caedmon, Saint, 137
Caldwell, Erskine, 150
Capote, Truman, 150

Carlyle, Thomas, 19, 22, 24, 27, 28, 31, 32, 33, 77, 101, 136
Cash, W. J., 34
Catton, Bruce, 34
Chaucer, Geoffrey, 135
Chesterfield, Lord, 104
Chivalry, 32–45, 62, 135–36
Chopin, Frederic, 106
Christ, 104, 122, 133, 134, 137, 138–140
Civil Rights Bill, 60, 80
Coleridge, Samuel Taylor, 149
Columbus, Christopher, 104, 147
Commager, Henry Steel, 80
Conner, Frederick, 102
Cowley, Abraham, 62
Crane, Stephen, 34

Damrosch, Leopold, 69
Dante Alighieri, 104, 137
De Bellis, Jack, 152
De Forest, John W., 32
Dickinson, Emily, 148
Donne, John, 148
Don Quixote (Cervantes), 34
Dream of Xmas (Heller), 71

"Each and All" (Emerson), 110
Eckenrode, H. J., 33
Egdon Heath, 117
Eliot, George, 97, 136
Ellick Garry in "9 from 8," 58
Emerson, Ralph Waldo, 27, 29, 36, 63, 101, 110, 111, 112, 116, 119, 126, 137, 148
Epictetus, 137
Eureka (Poe), 131
Evangeline (Longfellow), 78

87396

DATE DUE

GAYLORD			PRINTED IN U.S.A.